*HEREFORDSHIRE,
THE WELSH CONNECTION*

HEREFORDSHIRE, THE WELSH CONNECTION

Colin Lewis

© Text: Colin Lewis

*Copyright © by Gwasg Carreg Gwalch 2006.
All rights reserved. No part of this publication
may be reproduced, stored in a retrieval system,
or transmitted in any form or by any means, electronic,
electrostatic, magnetic tape, mechanical, photocopying,
recording, or otherwise, without prior permission
of the authors of the works herein.*

ISBN: 0-86381-958-3

Cover design: Sian Parri

*First published in 2006 by
Gwasg Carreg Gwalch, 12 Iard yr Orsaf, Llanrwst, Wales LL26 0EH
☎ 01492 642031   📠 01492 641502
✉ books@carreg-gwalch.co.uk   Internet: www.carreg-gwalch.co.uk*

*i'm annwyl wraig
Janette*

Contents

Introduction: My interest begins – Hereford in Wales – The Setting – The ancient kingdoms of Ergyng and Ewyas – the subject matter of this book.

Chapter 1. Caradog and the Silures: The Roman invasions – The Britons – The Romans – Invasion – Caradog – The Silures – Resistance – Roman remains – Was it worth it?

Chapter 2. Vortigern Earl of the Wye: The end of empire – Vortigern – The coming of the Saxons – The Legend of Emrys – How bad was Vortigern?

Chapter 3. The Saints came marching in: A new start – St Martin of Tours and the saints of Wales – St Dyfrig, Prince of the Wye – The settlements of the saints – The saints of Ewyas – St Beuno and the Tale of Winefride – The Forest of Dean.

Chapter 4. Attack and Counter Attack: Juggernaut – The Hermit King – Meurig – Ithel – Attacks on Ergyng – Pact.

Chapter 5. From Sea to Sea: The Mighty dyke – Offa – Lichfield – A bulwark against the Welsh – A story of Murder most foul – About Offa's Dyke – Wat's Dyke – Differences in Offa's frontier.

Chapter 6. The Overlords: The coming of the Vikings – Hywel the Good – King of the West – Friendship with Wessex – The great lawmaker – The Wye Frontier – Bishop Cyfeiliog – The Ordinance Concerning The Dunsaete.

Chapter 7. Gruffudd ap Llywelyn and the Borderlands: The Warrior King – The battle of Rhyd y Groes – King Edward and the Normans – The Battle of Hereford – The Peace of Billingsley – Gruffudd swears allegiance – Downfall and Aftermath – The incident of the Hunting Lodge – What could have been – Raids into Dean.

Chapter 8. Lords of the March: The conquest of Wales – The plan for Wales – The creation of the March – The condition of the borderland – Fitzosbern and the De Lacys – The nature of Norman settlement.

Chapter 9. The Twelfth Century: A battle for body and soul – Bishop Urban of Llandaf and his claim on Archenfield – The Book of Llandaf – Urban's enemies: Gerald the Welshman – Llanthony – The See of Llandaf – The Border – Gerald's story concerning the power of the Marcher Lords.

Chapter 10. Owain Glyndŵr: The fire burns bright – The course of the war – The Beginning – The fire spreads – Glyndŵr the statesman – The Tripartite Indenture – The French – Glyndŵr and Hereford – The last act – His final resting place.

Chapter 11. The Son of Prophecy: Duped – Henry VII, Wales and the March – Family origins – Wars of the Roses – Henry and Wales – The March of Wales – The Council of the Principality and March of Wales: Henry VIII and the Act of Union – Revolution – The Hanging Bishop – The Act of Union – A greater Herefordshire – Betrayal of trust.

Chapter 12. The Heritage: A rich Celtic Heritage – The Welsh Bible – Welsh Non-Conformity in the 17th and 18th centuries – The Drovers – The Welsh language in Ewyas, Archenfield and the Forest of Dean in the 18th and 19th centuries – Welsh Hereford into the 20th century.

Conclusion. The Heritage Today and Tomorrow: An ancient fear – The re-emergence of Wales – Rediscovering the Heritage.

Appendix 1. A Gazeteer of Welsh place-names in Archenfield and Ewyas.

Appendix 2. Examples of contemporary links between Wales and Hereford.

Introduction

Wales is the third part of this island, being on the left hand, near the middle of England, and in a similitude somewhat like to a turning down. It runneth forth within the ocean sea like to an half island, wherewith it is environed on all sides, saving on the east part, and there it boundeth on the river called Severn, which separates the Welsh and English people (albeit there are many writers of late time which limit Wales and England at the city of Hereford), adjudging that the beginning of Wales is at the town called Chepstow, the river named Wye, being increased with the river Lug, and flowing by Hereford, toucheth itself in the sea.

Polydore Vergil's English History, 1513

My interest begins

My interest in Herefordshire goes back a long way, all the way back to the time when I was still in school, a time when the strange expression 'Wales and Monmouthshire' was still in use. During a now vaguely remembered history lesson, one of my fellow pupils asked our teacher, Mr Morris, whether or not Monmouthshire was in Wales or England. Mr Morris replied that Monmouthshire was, and always had been in Wales, and that he would stake his life on the fact. Then, another boy asked, 'What about Herefordshire Sir?' Mr Morris paused, obviously wanting to get back to his lesson. Then, in reply he said, that yes, perhaps it had been in Wales long ago, but that it wasn't part of Wales any longer, and with that he ended any further discussion and returned to the lesson he'd been giving.

In spite of Mr Morris' somewhat unsatisfactory answer, from that day on, the boy's question stayed in my mind, and my interest in Herefordshire and the Borderlands of Wales had begun. It was an interest that was later, over the years, to lead me from Gloucester and the Forest of Dean to Chester, from Ross and the Wye Valley to Oswestry and to many places in between. Look at any good map, and you will see that whilst there is a scattering of Welsh names on the English side of the modern border, there are two areas in particular where the concentration of such names is much higher than anywhere else. These are the Oswestry area of Shropshire, and west of the Wye in Herefordshire. However, on my travels I found that although much had been written about Oswestry, with the people there generally seeming to be proud of their links with Wales, further south in Herefordshire, there appeared little awareness of any Welsh connection whatsoever. A state of affairs that this little book will, I hope, go some way to redress.

The more popular contemporary local guides, available in tourist offices and local shops, usually depicted the Welsh as wild alien raiders of the Middle Ages and, while not denying that there were any Welsh links at all in Herefordshire, they either tended to ignore them or say that any such links were pre-Saxon and very long ago. However, quite to the contrary, I found that this was definitely not the case, and even in the libraries of Hereford and Ross, I discovered that there were authors who wrote of 'Welsh Hereford', and that there was considerable evidence to show that not only did the Welsh element in Herefordshire survive the Saxon era, but that it also survived to the present day.

In the present day there are still some surprising links with Wales which are not mentioned in the tourist guides. For example the people of western Hereford must be familiar with the *Dŵr Cymru/Welsh Water* signs all over the place; this is because 'Welsh Water' is the 'water company' for the Wye basin and south-western Hereford. However, perhaps the most notable link with Wales is an ecclesiastical one, in that the entire county of Hereford is in fact in the Roman Catholic Archdiocese of Cardiff, which itself is part of the Church's Welsh Province.

***Note:** Details of other links will be found in the appendix.*

Hereford in Wales

Thus, whilst outwardly, modern Herefordshire might appear to be one of the most English of counties, I found that if you scratch the surface you'll find a rich Celtic heritage underneath. In fact, the Celtic heritage of Herefordshire compares favourably with that of the most Celtic of 'English counties', namely Cornwall, which many of its inhabitants count as a country in its own right.

In Cornwall today people are finding a new pride in their past, and there is a revival of all things Cornish, including the Cornish language. However, whilst Cornwall became part of Wessex in 936, there were parts of Hereford still in Wales 600 years later than that. Again, whilst the Cornish language is now enjoying a revival, it died out as an everyday spoken language in the 18th century. Yet there is good reason to believe that Welsh, the sister language of Cornish, was still spoken as a native language of Herefordshire into the 20th century.

Throughout the Middle Ages, Herefordshire was a frontier county, and the expression 'Hereford in Wales' was common on official documents. Whether this referred to the whole of the county or only to the western parts is not clear. Probably the latter, acknowledging that certain areas, west of the Wye, although administered by the county of Hereford, were in fact still in Wales. However, besides these areas, much of what is now western Herefordshire was still in the March of Wales, independently controlled by Marcher Lords up until 1536.

The setting

Although this book is mainly concerned with that part of Herefordshire which lies to the south and west of the Wye, both the city of Hereford and the market town of Ross, in particular, are important focal points for this area. It was also sometimes essential for me to include other parts of the county as well, especially in the west and along the Wye Valley itself. Again, there were times when I couldn't help but slip over into the lovely Forest of Dean as this is not only bordered by the Wye, but being west of the River Severn and separated from the rest of Gloucester does, together with western Herefordshire, form the Southern Borderland of the March.

The ancient kingdoms of Ergyng and Ewyas

Look at a map of Herefordshire, and you will see that the south-west part of the county is bound by the River Wye in the east and the north, and by the modern Welsh border in the west. This area was once the home of the two ancient Welsh kingdoms of EWYAS, which was in the hilly north-western corner and ERGYNG, which lay along the banks of the Wye and to the south of Ewyas, and was the larger and more fertile of the two. At one time, Ergyng must have extended further east, as the name 'ERGYNG' was itself derived from the name of the old Roman town of ARICONIUM, at Weston Under Penyard near Ross. Indeed, a former loop in the Wye once included both Ross and Ariconium on the western bank of the Wye. Another change in the course of the river also appears to have cut off the Kings Caple district from Ergyng.

Although Ewyas kept its name through the ages it was later split in two, to become the lordships of Ewyas Lacy and Ewyas Harold. The English changed Ergyng to Archenfield (from the same Roman root), in the early Middle Ages, and then again changed this, with some boundary adjustments, to Wormelow in the later Middle Ages. With this change the northern part of Ergyng became the hundred of Webtree. However, although finally conquered by the Saxons and Normans in the 11th century, these little kingdoms were to retain their Welshness for many centuries to come.

The subject matter of this book

Although this book uses historical sources for its subject matter, it is not just a local history of south-western Herefordshire. It unashamedly portrays a Welsh viewpoint, and is, as the title suggests, mainly concerned with the county's 'Welsh Connection'. Consequently, although its story ranges from the Roman invasion up to the present day, I believe the incidents that it depicts will show how central and influential Herefordshire's contribution to Welsh history has really been.

For example:

- In the first century AD, western Hereford was in the territory of the Silures of southern Wales. These held the might of Rome at bay for thirty years.
- In the 5th and 6th centuries, during 'the Age of Saints', it has been said that Herefordshire was the cradle of Welsh Christianity.
- In 1063, it was the war to secure the Wye Frontier at Hereford that led to the downfall of one of Wales' greatest rulers, Gruffudd ap Llywelyn. His death fragmented Welsh unity on the very eve of the Norman invasion.
- In 1067 William Fitzosbern, the new Norman Earl of Hereford, launched his invasion of the southern March of Wales.
- In the 15th century, the county was not only the scene of several battles in Owain Glyndŵr's War of Welsh Independence, but also became his last resting place.
- In the 17th and 18th centuries, western Hereford played a vital role in the Welsh Nonconformist Movement.

In keeping with the general theme of this story, most of the central characters portrayed are either Welsh or have a strong Welsh connection, and although I've tried to concentrate only on Herefordshire, both the need for explanation and my own interest in the unfolding narrative have sometimes carried me elsewhere.

Colin Lewis, July 2003

Booklist:

Polydore Vergil's English History, Vol.1, (circa 1513, pages 11-13), ed. Sir Henry Ellis. A Llanerch facsimile reprint of the Camden Soc. Edition of 1846.

Catholic Directory and Year Book 2002, Published by the Authority of the Bishops of Wales, General Editor, Pastoral Resources Centre, Cardiff.

Coming Down the Wye, by Robert Gibbings, pub. by J.M. Dent & Sons Ltd., London.

Chapter 1

Caradog and the Silures

The Roman invasions

After his conquest of Gaul in 58BC, Julius Caesar turned his attention to Britain, which he invaded twice, once in 55BC and again, the following year, in 54BC. His intention, however, was not conquest, but rather to punish the Britons for the help they had given to their fellow Celts, the Gauls, in their resistance to Caesar. He never intended to occupy Britain. Thus having bloodied the natives, he returned to Gaul, after being promised tribute from the defeated Britons.

In complete contrast, the invasion ordered by the emperor Claudius in 43AD was clearly intended to conquer Britain. However, the Britons enjoyed their own way of life and, fiercely opposed the invasion. One Briton in particular stood out as a leader in this fight to stay free. His name was Caratacus, or as he is better known in Wales, Caradog. For 8 years he led the fierce Silures of southern Wales in their defence of the Wye Frontier, and it was the Silures who almost ruined the Roman plan of conquest.

The Britons

At the time of the Claudian invasion in 43AD, Britain was divided amongst various Celtic tribes. In the far north of Scotland, there were the wild and mysterious Picts, in southern Scotland and the west of Britain, the various tribes of the Britons, and in the south and east, the more technologically advanced kingdoms of the Belgae, a people who although closely related to the Britons in culture and language had migrated from Gaul (France and Belgium) over the previous century, and were actively engaged in extending their power and influence in the north and west. Unlike the tribes of the north and the west, the Belgae had a monetary system and their own coinage, based on Roman designs. The richest and most powerful of the Belgic kingdoms was that of the Catuvellauni, whose territory lay north of the Thames and stretched from the Chiltern Hills to their capital, Colchester and the Essex coast. Their king, Cunobelinus (Shakespeare's *Cymbeline*) had been acknowledged as the most powerful 'King of the Britons' by the other tribes of southern Britain.

There were two main tribes in what is now Herefordshire, the Silures, west of the River Wye and the Decangi occupying land between the Wye and the Severn, although in the north of this area was the territory of the Cornovii of Shropshire, and the south was probably controlled by the Silures. There is evidence at Lydney that the Silures occupied The Forest of Dean. To the east of the Severn were the Belgic Dobunni, who were subject to the Catuvellauni. Under Roman rule, The Forest became, administratively, part of Dobunni territory run from Cirencester.

The Romans

When Caesar led his raids, he knew little of Britain, except that it was a strange mist shrouded island on the edge of the world, whose inhabitants had helped the enemies of Rome in Gaul. Besides, the Romans had only recently conquered Gaul and had their hands full consolidating their hold there.

However, in the hundred years since Caesar's invasion, trade between Britain and Roman Gaul had flourished, with Roman goods finding a ready market in lowland Britain. In exchange, Britain exported corn, slaves, hides and metals such as gold, iron, copper, tin and lead. Trade was helped by the introduction of a coinage based on that of Rome itself, but with the impressed images of local Celtic rulers. However, the Romans wouldn't remain satisfied with having Britain as a trading partner only, and reports of Britain's wealth brought back by Roman traders and merchants caused the rulers of the Empire to cast increasingly greedy eyes towards the island on the edge of the world.

For over ninety years, Rome had traded with Britain, and both the emperors Augustus and Tiberius were satisfied with Britain's client status and concentrated on improving the empire's defences on the Rhine in order to hold back the fierce German tribes in the dark, dank forests beyond. Then, after 37AD everything changed. Tiberius died and was succeeded by the infamous Caligula. A year or so later, Cunobelinus, 'King of the Britons' died, leaving dissention among his sons regarding his succession. Two of his sons, Caradog and Togodumnus had inherited the kingdom, with a third son, Adminius being driven out, either by Cunobelinus himself before his death, or by his brothers. He fled, and sought the protection and aid of Rome. Thus, in 40AD on the pretext that he was helping Admius, the emperor Caligula prepared an invasion fleet at Boulogne. However, his mutinous army refused to board the ships. So, it was probably with contempt for his army, and not because he was insane, that he then told these same troops to collect seashells instead. The following year he was murdered by another group of mutinous soldiers, his own bodyguard.

He was succeeded by Claudius, who adopted Caligula's project with enthusiasm. Claudius was inspired by the example of Julius Caesar. However, where Julius had only raided Britain, Claudius intended to conquer it, so that he would be the greater. Another excuse to invade soon presented itself, when the territory of Verica, king of the Atrebates, a tribe in what is now southern Surrey and Essex, was overrun by the sons of Cunobelin. Verica immediately appealed to Rome for help.

Claudius was better than Caligula at handling people, and he knew how to delegate authority. He chose an able general, Aulus Plautius, to command the expedition. However, the troops were still nervous about embarking, and had to be reassured by Claudius' close friend, the former slave, Narcissus. It is said that soon after mounting the rostrum to address the troops, Narcissus had them roaring with laughter, thus breaking the tension. What could have been a mutiny dissolved in laughter, and soon the men were on their ships and underway. Consequently, possibly in the spring or early summer of 43AD, four legions, each of 6,000 hardened veterans from the Rhine frontier, and auxiliaries, including cavalry, about 50,000 men all told, set sail in three separate squadrons of ships, in order to make three separate landfalls.

Invasion

The probable landing area for the invading fleet was at Richborough, on the river Stour, near Ramsgate. Plautius was amazed that the Britons didn't oppose him in force on the beaches. After the landing both Togodumnus and Caradog led attacks against the invaders, with little effect. The Romans, following the route that Caesar had taken, drove the Britons back to the River Medway, where they managed to regroup.

Now, with the forces of the Britons massed on the west bank of the Medway, the Romans, rather than spend time building a fleet of boats to cross the river, used a special force of Batavi (Germanic auxiliaries), who were trained to swim in full battle kit, to cross upstream of the Britons in order to attack them from the rear. The main force was now able to bridge and cross the river with less opposition. The ensuing battle was hard fought and lasted two days. In the end, the Britons were forced to retreat to the Thames, which they crossed in the vicinity of London Bridge. The Romans, again using the Batavi and building a bridge, caught the Britons in a pincer movement in which they suffered heavy losses. Following this, the Romans advanced on the Catuvellaunian capital, Camulodunum, near modern Colchester, and were resisted in numerous skirmishes en route. It was during one of these encounters that Togodumnus was killed. Caradog, now realising that the battle in the south-east of Britain was lost for the time being at least, retired with his family to the west in order to continue the fight on more defendable ground. Here, he was welcomed as a war leader by the fierce tribe of the Silures who lived beyond the Wye.

In the meantime, Claudius had arrived just in time to make a show of entering Camulodunum as the great, triumphant Conqueror of Britain. He only stayed a short while before returning to Rome, leaving Plautius to complete the conquest. However, although the Romans easily conquered the lowlands of Britain, with many tribes, such as the Dobunni of Gloucester, submitting without a fight, the less sophisticated tribes of the west were much more resistant. These not only defended their own territory, but also, under Caradog, attacked by raiding across the Severn, deep into Roman held territory. The Romans soon came to realise that the only way to remove the threat of a counter offensive by the Britons was to conquer Wales, the centre of resistance to their rule.

Caradog

Although the tribal organisation of the Silures was quite informal when compared with the Belgae, they were still able to act with considerable unity in time of war, when they followed the Celtic practice of appointing a war leader. In disputes with neighbouring tribes the leader would usually be one of their own best warriors, of proven prowess. In the exceptional circumstances of the Roman invasion, the Silures obviously regarded Caradog's experience of leadership as more important than the fact that he was a prince of another tribe, the Belgic Catuvellauni. He already had experience of fighting the Romans and had proven his valour on the banks of the Medway and the Thames.

One can imagine the warrior Silures, who although feared by their enemies were renowned for their hospitality, inviting the richly dressed prince Caradog into their rough homes to join them in drinking mead and telling ribald stories around the warmth of their fires. In normal times, family and clan came before tribal matters, but now, in the face of the terrible Roman threat to their freedom and way of life, they were united in their loyalty to their new war chief, from another tribe.

Leading the Silures, Caradog was not only able to defend the Wye frontier for eight long years, but he also managed to mount raids into Roman held territory. One large raid was recorded in the autumn of 47AD, shortly after the arrival of Ostorius Scapula as Governor of Britain. Although this raid was repulsed, it showed that the hostile Silurians, under Caradog, could penetrate deep into Roman-controlled territory. Consequently, Ostorius's response was to consolidate what had already been gained by pouring troops into a line of fortifications from Seaton on the Devon coast, through Cirencester and Leicester to Lincoln, and connected by the Fosse Way. This line was intended to act as a temporary frontier in order to protect those friendly tribes who had submitted to Rome, and from which the Romans could mount further attacks into hostile territory.

Although, by the following year, Ostorius felt confident enough to advance the 14th and 20th Legions to set up a base at Wroxeter, Caradog and his Silures were still causing considerable problems with their attacks on the forts of the Fosse Way. To counter this, Ostorius established a military fort at Gloucester (Glevum), in 50AD. This was manned by the 2nd Legion, and was to secure the lower Severn Valley and act as the main forward base for operations against the Silures.

Caradog, now finding himself prevented from advancing in the south by the 2nd Legion, must have been concerned by the presence of two legions in the upper Severn Valley at Wroxeter. Could this be the prelude to a massive pincer move intended to destroy the

Britons' resistance? At the very least, the Romans at Wroxeter would have cut any links that the Welsh tribes had with the northern England tribe of the Brigantes, whom Caradog saw as possible allies. Consequently, at this point, he left the Silures to continue their guerrilla war in the south, and moved north to lead the Ordovices, another fierce Welsh tribe of Mid Wales.

Whatever the reason, whether he felt confident of winning or was desperate to break the Roman stranglehold, he risked open battle with the most powerful army in the world. However, it was at a place of his choosing, somewhere on the banks of the upper Severn. Before the battle Tacitus quotes him as telling his warriors, 'that this was the day, this was the battle, which would either win back their freedom or enslave them forever'. Every man swore by his tribal oath that no enemy weapons, no wounds, would make them yield.

Yet, it all was to no avail. The Roman soldiers crossed the river without difficulty, reached the Britons' ramparts and, in spite of the hail of missiles, advanced under a roof of locked shields to demolish Caradog's defences and win the day. Caradog escaped but his wife and family were captured. He now fled north to the land of the Brigantes, hoping for their support to fight the invaders, but Cartimandua, the queen of the Brigantes, had now submitted to the Romans and become their client ruler. She arrested Caradog and gave him to the Romans in chains.

Caradog and his family and chief followers were taken to Rome to be paraded in front of emperor and people. By now Caradog's reputation for resistance had spread throughout the empire and Claudius needed to humiliate him publicly before executing him. In the parade, his wife, daughter, brothers and lieutenants 'degraded themselves by entreaties', but Caradog did not even bow his head, let alone beg for mercy. Instead, according to Tacitus, he said:

> *Had my lineage and rank been accompanied by only moderate success, I should have come to this city as a friend rather than prisoner, and you would not have distained to ally yourself peacefully with one so nobly born, the ruler of so many nations. As it is, humiliation is my lot, glory yours. I had horses, men, arms, wealth. Are you surprised I am sorry to lose them? If you want to rule the world, does it follow that everyone else welcomes enslavement? If I had surrendered without a blow before being brought before you, neither my downfall nor your triumph would have become famous. If you execute me, they will be forgotten. Spare me, and I shall be an everlasting token of your mercy!*

translated by Michael Grant (Penguin Classics)

Claudius responded by pardoning him and the others, and freeing them on condition that they remain in exile in Rome for the rest of their lives.

The Silures

The Silures were not the typical fair-headed Celtic types described by the Classical writers. They were less civilised than the tribes to the east of them, but more intrepid and indomitable. The Roman historian Tacitus believed that they looked more like the swarthy faced, curly headed Iberians of Spain, which appears to indicate that they were a pre-Celtic people, who had adopted the more advanced culture of the Britons, along with the Brythonic language, which later developed into Welsh.

Although the hill-fort was the most common feature

of Celtic Britain, the Silurian design was distinctive enough to make their forts easily identifiable. They were often smaller than those in other parts of Britain, more like enclosed farms than major fortifications. Also, the entrances were different in that the ramparts forming the entrance passageways were funnelled from wide on the outside and narrow at the entrance gate. This confined any attackers and made them an easy target for the defenders' stones and spears.

From their hill-fort design, we find that the Silures occupied an area that was mainly south and west of the River Wye, and east of the River Tywi in Carmarthen. It included Gwent, Glamorgan, the western part of Hereford, eastern Carmarthen and much of Brecon. However, in certain areas their control appears to have extended beyond this, as is shown by the fact that mineral springs near Llandrindod Wells were called 'Balnea Silures' (Silurian Baths) by the Romans, and the name 'Silvlanvs' in the temple of Nodens at Lydney Park in The Forest of Dean, equates with the word Silure and should be read 'Silulanus', according to professor John Rees. Also, Nodens was a sea or water god worshipped by the Silures.

In his *History of Gwent* Dr Raymond Howell believes that the Silures, at times, pursued expansionist policies and he points to the fact that their largest hill-forts were on the borders of their territory. Y Gaer Fawr is in the Tywi valley, Spital Meend on the eastern bank of the Wye, not far from Tidenham, and Twyn y Gaer (near Symond's Yat), which appears to have been captured from the Decangi tribe of Herefordshire.

The tribal capital of the Silures appears to have been the large hill-fort at Llanmelin, as it was near here, at Caerwent that the Romans later built the regional capital for Siluria, Venta Silurium. Also, Llanmelin was not far from another large hill-fort at Sudbrook, which was the main port for Silurian trade with the West Country.

Resistance

Although Caradog was defeated in 51AD, any hope the Romans had that this would end the war was soon abandoned. Both the Silures and the Ordovices fought on. The Silures in particular, being, as Tacitus puts it, 'exceptionally stubborn', repeatedly defeated Roman forces entering Silurian territory and forced them to flee for their lives. One large force was cut off near Clyro, close to Hay on Wye, and lost a prefect, eight centurions and many men, before being rescued by a relief force. More Roman defeats were to follow. Shortly after Caradog's capture, Ostorius sent two auxiliary cohorts, over a thousand soldiers in all, into Silurian territory, only to see them trapped and captured by the Silures who then sold their prisoners as slaves to other tribes. The Silures were becoming the leaders of resistance to the Romans and they encouraged the other tribes to join them. At this stage, Ostorius said that the whole tribe must be utterly exterminated but this only enraged the Silures and spurred them on to greater effort. Then, Ostorius died suddenly, because, according to Tacitus, he 'was exhausted by his anxious responsibilities'. Although the Silures hadn't actually killed him in battle, the strain of the protracted campaign against them had. His entire time as governor had been a period of constant warfare with the tribes of Wales, during which the Romans had suffered heavy losses difficult to justify against the gains made.

The emperor Claudius wasted no time in sending a

new governor, Aulus Didius Gallus. However, by the time he arrived later in 52AD an even greater disaster had befallen the Romans. The Silures had actually met and defeated a full legion, probably the 20th. (Legio XX) and followed this with widespread raids.

On the death of Claudius in 54AD, the situation had become so bad as the military and economic costs spiralled upwards, that Nero, the new emperor even considered withdrawing his forces from Britain altogether. But, in the end, he decided to keep them there, because to do otherwise would tarnish the honour of Rome and the memory of Claudius.

Back in Britain, Didius realised that there could be no swift victory, and so settled for a policy of containment and modest advancement where this was possible. However, although by 60AD the Silures were safely contained and encircled by a series of auxiliary forts, it would be another 18 years before they were conquered. Eventually, in 78AD, Julius Frontinus, who had become Governor of Britain in 75AD, was able to turn his full attention to the Silures and defeat them with a massive frontal attack, and by using his navy to land troops at their rear. The Ordovices were conquered in the same year by Frontinus's successor, Julius Agricola. That tribe had almost annihilated a cavalry regiment stationed on the borders, and the response from the new governor was swift and terrible. He mounted a massive expedition from the newly founded Chester and almost wiped out the Ordovices in an orgy of blood.

Roman remains

The nature of the Roman occupation west of the Severn for the next 320 years or so can be seen in the ruins they left behind or, perhaps more significantly, the ruins that they didn't leave. There were plenty of forts and there were fortified towns with a network of roads to connect them all but there were very few villas to indicate civilian farming activity. Those that have been found are mainly in the Forest of Dean and the coastal strips of Glamorgan and Gwent. However, even those found in the Forest might well have been the private homes of officials concerned with iron mining and smelting and not farming villas at all.

In his *Historical Atlas of Wales*, William Rees writes that a line could be drawn from Flamborough Head in Yorkshire to near Exeter in Devon, dividing Britain into the Civil Zone to the south and east of this line and the Military Zone to the north and west of it. The distribution of Roman villas is very sparse north and west of this line. Although the Romans did attempt to 'civilise' the Military Zone with the establishment of civilian cities as tribal civitas (capitals), they were mainly interested in maintaining the security of the Civil Zone, whilst at the same time exploiting any resources in the Military Zone.

The towns

Iron ore was mined extensively in the Forest of Dean and processed in the nearby towns of Abergavenny (Gobannium, meaning 'the place of the blacksmiths'), Monmouth (Blestium), Trelech, Usk and Ariconium (Weston-under-Penyard, near Ross). It was from the name of Ariconium that the later names of Ergyng and Archenfield for the district south-west of Hereford were derived.

The massive military presence in the area is evidenced by the legionary fortress at Caerleon (Isca, founded by Frontinus in 75AD during the closing stages of the

Silurian War), the fortified town of Kenchester (Magna Castra, near Hereford), and the numerous forts throughout the former Silurian territory. All these settlements and forts were linked by an excellent system of roads.

The roads

A road ran from Gloucester (Glevum), through the Forest of Dean, crossing the Wye at Chepstow and on to Caerwent and Caerleon. From Caerleon, one road ran west along the line of the present A48, past the forts of Cowbridge (Bovium, which was also a market centre for the Vale of Glamorgan), Neath (Nidum) and on to Carmarthen which, as Maridunum, was the only other tribal civitas (for the Demetae tribe) west of the Severn. From Carmarthen the road ran north to Segontium (Caernarfon). Another road from Caerleon went in a northerly direction, passing Usk, Abergavenny, and through the lower part of the Golden Valley on its way to Kenchester, Wigmore, Wroxeter and Chester. Other roads linked with Monmouth, Brecon and so on, making a comprehensive network that joined all the forts and settlements.

Was it worth it?

At the time of the Claudian invasion, Britain was a friendly client state of the empire and the already strong trading links were growing stronger. Not only that, but the tribes of the south-east were, increasingly, adopting Roman customs from their Belgic cousins in Gaul. Had this situation been allowed to continue, it is possible that this part of Britain at least, would have been well on the way to being Romanised by the 2nd century, and Rome would have been getting all the resources it wanted through peaceful trade, without needing to invade. As it was, although the conquest of the lowlands went smoothly enough, the cost of creating and maintaining safe frontiers in the north and west of Britain possibly outweighed any profit Rome could have made from Britain. Also, there was the matter of Claudius taking four legions from the Rhine Frontier. This was where Rome's real enemies lay in wait, in the great Dark Forest of Germany. Ultimately, it was from this Dark Forest that Rome's nemesis came. Claudius might have been better advised to focus the might of Rome in that direction, rather than attack a friendly neighbour.

Note: There is a strong local tradition that the 16th century country mansion near Sellack church (map reference 56.27), now called 'Caradoc' but formerly 'Caradoc Court' and before that 'Caer Caradoc, was built near the site of a hill-fort that was Caradog's bastion, defending the Wye from Roman invasion.

Booklist:
Roman Britain, 55BC-AD400, by Malcolm Todd, pub. Fontana Paperbacks, London, 1985.
The Great Invasion, by Leonard Cottrell, pub. Evans Brothers Limited, London, 1963.
A History of Gwent, by Raymond Howell, pub. Gomer Press, Llandysul, Dyfed, 1988.
Tacitus, The Annals of Imperial Rome, translated by Michael Grant, pub. Penguin Books, 1961.
Tacitus, on Britain and Germany, a translation of the 'Agricola' and the 'Germania' by H. Mattingly, pub Penguin Books, 1948.
Roman Britain, by R.R. Sellman, pub. Methuen, London, 1963.

Romans in Britain, by Rodney Legg, pub. Heinemann, London, 1983.

An Historical Atlas of Wales, by William Rees, pub. Faber and Faber Ltd., London, 1972.

A Map of Roman Britain, third edition, pub. by The Ordinance Survey, Chessington, Surrey, 1956.

Celtic Wales, a pocket guide, by Miranda Green and Ray Howell, pub. Cardiff University of Wales Press/The Western Mail, 2000.

South Wales, A Geographia Guide, 114 Fleet Street, London.

Through Welsh Border Country, by Mark Richards, pub. Thornhill Press, Cheltenham, 1978.

Chapter 2

Vortigern, Earl of the Wye

The end of empire

*The Gauls too, we have been told, had their hour of military glory;
but then came decadence with peace, and valour went the way of lost liberty.
The same fate has befallen such of the Britons as have long been conquered;
the rest are still what the Gauls used to be.*

Tacitus, in his *Agricola*

By 410AD the Romans had gone, and although the semi-independent Brythonic tribes of the north and west had never forgotten how to defend themselves, the thoroughly Romanised Britons of the south in the Civil Zone were almost helpless without the army to protect them. Now the Irish in the west, the Picts in the north and the Saxons in the east saw their opportunity and fell upon the towns and cities of southern Britain, looting, burning and mercilessly killing the unfortunate inhabitants.

For decades the beleaguered Britons managed to hold their ground but in the middle of the fifth century, supposedly because of the treachery of one man who, according to the 12th century historian, Geoffrey of Monmouth, came from the Wye Valley area, there came a larger more determined invasion of pagan Saxons. They hated everything Roman, including the Latin language and the new state religion, Christianity. The traitor is said to have been the morally decadent king of Britain, Vortigern, who is reported as betraying his people because of his lust for a Saxon woman.

Vortigern

As the Romans went back home, there eagerly emerged from the coracles that had carried them across the sea, the foul hordes of Scots (Irish) and Picts, like dark throngs of worms who wriggle out of fissures when the sun is high and the weather warm. They were to some extent different in their customs, but in perfect accord in their greed for bloodshed.

Gildas (in his *The Ruin of Britain*, circa 540AD)

After suffering terrible losses, compounded by plague and famine, the leaders of the Britons appealed to Rome for help, saying that the barbarians pushed them to the sea, and the sea pushed them back to the barbarians and that between the two kinds of death they were either drowned or slaughtered. Gildas says *that the Britons begged for help from Rome, like frightened chicks huddling under the wings of their faithful parents*. But Rome was in no position to help, and could only advise the Britons to look to their own defence.

Many of the Britons died, whilst others fled as refugees to Wales and across the sea to Brittany which had been colonised with Britons. Yet some, based in the hills and the woods, stayed to fight and after years of losing ground eventually began to drive their enemies back. Geoffrey of Monmouth writes that the Britons appealed for help from their fellow countrymen in Brittany and that the king there sent his younger brother, Constantine, with an army to drive the barbarians back on condition that he became king of Britain.

Geoffrey says that Constantine proved to be a good ruler and was called both the 'Defender' and the 'Blessed'. He had three sons called Constans, Ambrosius (the 'Emrys' of Welsh legend) and Uther. However, after ruling Britain for sixteen peaceful years, he was assassinated by a vengeful Pict and was succeeded firstly by Constans and then, in dubious circumstances, by his brother-in-law Vortigern.

Nennius, a 9th century historian, says that Vortigern was of noble descent, having family associations with the ruling families of Gloucester and Mid Wales. Geoffrey adds that he married Severa, Constantine's sister, possibly in order to strengthen his claim to the throne. Geoffrey specifically links him to the Wye Valley area, as the Earl of Gwent, Ergyng/Archenfield and Ewyas. However, in spite of his noble origin, Vortigern is always seen in a bad light and portrayed as an ambitious, unscrupulous man who betrayed his country. In keeping with this villainous image, it is alleged that he arranged for a group of Picts to murder Constans, the new king, in order for him to seize power.

When the Picts brought Constans's head to him, Vortigern is said to have burst into tears. Yet, this was only pretence. He'd never really been happier in his life. The guardians of the two younger brothers, now fearing for their charges' lives, fled with them to Brittany where the king is said to have given them a princely upbringing. In the meantime, Vortigern is reported to have been constantly dreading the possibility of their return to claim their kingdom.

The coming of the Saxons 449AD

Although the Britons had driven the invaders away, this was to prove to be only a temporary respite. Following Constantine's death, a plague weakened the Britons' defences and the same old enemies, seized their opportunity and returned in even greater force. Thus the council of elders, presided over by Vortigern, who Gildas calls the 'Proud Tyrant', decided, according to Roman traditional practice, to employ German mercenaries in order to defeat their enemies. However, this course of action was to prove disastrous. Gildas says, that *'the council together with the Proud Tyrant were struck blind'*, deciding that *'the ferocious Saxons, hated by man and God, should be let into our island like wolves into the fold'* in order to defeat the northerners.

The Saxons, under the leadership of Hengest and Horsa, were to be paid in land and supplies, and were granted the Isle of Thanet in the north-east corner of Kent. However, to drive the Picts and Irish back, they sent to Germany for reinforcements. Consequently, with their numbers increased, they began to demand more land and supplies. However, the initial reaction of the Britons was to tell them to go away, that their help was no longer needed. The elders of the Saxons then met to decide whether to make war on the Britons.

But Nennius writes that Hengest was a shrewd and skilful man of experience and he knew how militarily weak the Britons were. Thus, instead of complying and taking his men back to Germany, Hengest was able to persuade Vortigern that he actually needed more Saxons to fight the northerners. So, with the king's agreement, Hengest sent across the sea for another sixteen ships full of warriors. In one of these ships was Hengest's beautiful daughter, whom Geoffrey calls Rowena.

No sooner had the ships arrived than Hengest arranged a banquet for Vortigern, where Rowena was to serve the wine. Everyone got drunk, including Vortigern who became so infatuated with Rowena that he offered up to half his kingdom for her hand in marriage. Hengest quickly consulted with his elders, and together they decided to ask for the whole of Kent. The drunken, love smitten Vortigern readily agreed to their request. But he had no right to do this without first consulting his own people. The ruler of Kent, Gwyrangen, wasn't even informed that his kingdom had been handed over to the heathens.

Naturally, the Britons resisted the attempted Saxon takeover of Kent and in the war that followed, they fought under the leadership of Vortimer, Vortigern's son, who killed Horsa in battle and drove the Saxons back to Thanet before being killed himself, poisoned by his step mother Rowena, according to Geoffrey.

Now the Saxons brought more men from Germany and Hengest asked for a meeting of both sides to be arranged in order to arrive at a peaceful settlement. The representatives of the two sides were supposed to be unarmed but the Saxons had hidden weapons, and at a call of *'English draw your knives'* from Hengest, they treacherously massacred the leaders of the Britons, sparing only Vortigern who was made to hand over half of his kingdom.

After this, the fight was led by Ambrosius, who, Gildas says, was the greatest of the Britons' leaders and believed him to have been the last great Roman, 'born of the purple'. According to Geoffrey, Ambrosius and Uther had returned from exile in Brittany to hunt down Vortigern, who had fled to his castle of Ganarew, in Ergyng/Archenfield. There the brothers caught up with him and burnt the castle about him.

Next, Ambrosius is said to have killed Hengest in battle. He made the defeated English agree to be his vassals and granted them land close to the Scottish border. However, the peace was not to last. The English sent to Germany for more reinforcements and continued their advance only to be stopped again by Ambrosius at the first battle of Badon Hill (possibly near Swindon), in 493, according to Bede in his *Ecclesiastical History of the English People* (written 731AD).

At this point, Geoffrey says that Ambrosius was poisoned by an Englishman disguised as a physician and that his brother Uther was left to carry on the fight.

According to Geoffrey, after Ambrosius' death a mysterious omen was seen in the sky. A great comet appeared, the multiple tail of which made it resemble a dragon's head. Taking this as a sign, Uther is then said to have had a banner made showing a dragon's head and to have adopted the surname 'Pendragon', which means 'dragon's head'. However, after leading the Britons of southern Wales and the West Country in the war against the English under his dragon banner, he too was murdered by them, drinking poisoned water from a well at Verulam (St Albans). Uther was now succeeded by his fifteen year old son, the legendary Arthur who fought many battles against the English, culminating in his victory at the second Battle of Badon Hill in 516AD which halted the English advance for fifty years.

The Legend of Emrys

One of the traditional stories that Nennius retells concerns a wondrous boy and a prophecy.

One day, Vortigern's wizards, who always advised him, told him that the English whom he'd invited into his kingdom had turned against him and that he should go to one of the furthest corners of his realm and there build a safe stronghold for himself. So, the king and his wizards decided to go to Snowdon where they found a site that appeared to be suitable for a fortress.

Building went well for a while, then one morning when the builders came to the site they were shocked to find that the fortress and all the building materials had disappeared during the night. This happened three times. The now perplexed Vortigern summoned his wizards for their advice. They told him that he must find a child with no father, kill him and then sprinkle his blood on the building site. What they told him seemed strange but he'd always relied on them in the past. So he sent them in search of a boy child without a father.

In Glamorgan, the wizards saw some boys playing with a ball and overheard them quarrelling. One boy said that the other was no good because he didn't have a father. On hearing this, the wizards questioned the boys and then went to the home of the one said to be fatherless. There, the boy's mother swore that she'd never been with a man. So they took the boy to Vortigern.

When he arrived at Vortigern's camp, the boy asked why he'd been brought there. Vortigern explained to him that unless he was killed and his blood sprinkled around the site of the fortress, it could not be built. The boy was astounded and demanded to know who'd said this to the king. When Vortigern told him that it was his wizards' advice, the boy asked to see them.

When they came, the boy wanted to know why it was necessary to sprinkle his blood on the site and how they had found this information. When they refused to answer, the boy told Vortigern that he knew why the fortress couldn't be built and would later explain in full but first he wanted to teach the wizards a lesson. The king agreed that he would like to get to the truth of the matter and so let the boy continue.

The boy asked the wizards if they knew what was under the foundations. When they shook their heads he told them that if they were to dig there, they would find a lake. As the wizards dug, the earth fell into a hole under which was a lake. The boy then asked them what was in the lake but they did not know. He showed them a jar in the lake and asked if they could guess as to its contents. Again the wizards were blank faced, so he told them to open the jar. Inside the jar there was a piece of folded cloth. He instructed them to carefully open the cloth. Wrapped in the cloth were two sleeping worms, one white and one red. When the worms awoke, they began to fight, one pushing the other towards the edge of the cloth, first the white, then the red. Three times the white worm pushed the red to the edge, then, on the fourth clash, the red worm drove the white off the cloth and across the lake. The cloth now vanished. When the boy asked the wizards if they knew what this meant, they were unable to provide an answer. So the boy began to explain.

The cloth, he said represented the kingdom of Britain, and the two worms were two dragons. The red dragon belonged to the Britons but the white dragon belonged to the English people who had seized so much of the kingdom of Britain. They would rule from sea to sea, but later, the Britons would rise up and valiantly throw the English back across the sea.

He then told them that they could never build the fortress there. They should go elsewhere but he would stay. Vortigern then asked the boy what his name was. The boy replied *'I am Ambrosius, that is Emrys, the Overlord'*. When the king asked about his family, Emrys told him that his father was one of the Consuls of the Roman People. So the king gave him the fortress and the western part of Britain and went with his wizards to the north where he built a city called 'Caer Gwrtheyrn' (Vortigern's Fortress).

In Geoffrey's later rendering of the story the boy's first name is Merlin and he is a different person from the Ambrosius who fought at Badon Hill. Merlin, as we all know, was destined to be the greatest wizard of all.

How bad was Vortigern?

When he was hated for his sin of receiving the English people by all men of his own nation, he wandered from place to place until at last his heart broke, and he died without honour. Others say that the earth opened and swallowed him on the night when his fortress was burnt about him.

Nennius

Following the collapse of Roman rule, Britain entered a Dark Age when countless people died violent deaths and whole cities went up in flames. Accurate records were lost in the terrible holocaust and only tales told at campfires survived, to be written down in a later age. The semi legendary stories that do come down to us may obscure some of the actual facts of fifth century Britain.

Thus, although none of the historians have a good word for Vortigern, it is possible that they, and especially Geoffrey, have been unfair to him. All the historians were monks who saw Vortigern as a thoroughly immoral person and because of the lack of reliable contemporary records it may have simplified matters for them to make him the scapegoat for the ruin of Britain.

Yet, as regards the hiring of Germanic mercenaries, Vortigern was in fact only following standard Roman practice, which had worked for centuries. Again, on the matter of his inviting the Saxons into Britain, there is ample evidence of a strong Germanic presence in Britain throughout the Roman period, including Saxon settlements on the east coast during the late Empire.

However, most of these Germans would not have been settlers, but auxiliaries in the Roman Army itself and, as such, based in all the major towns and cities of Roman Britain. Many of them would not have left with the legions by 410. So it is easy to imagine them rebelling and seizing towns and cities and looting when their normal income ceased with the collapse of Roman rule. When the Britons gave them land and supplies it may not only have been to enlist them against the Picts and Irish, but it could also have been the only way in which an already hard-pressed people could, as a temporary measure, buy the Germans off. Later, when the Britons were more organised and able to mount their own counter-offensives, it would be logical for the rebels to combine with their fellow Germans, the Saxon pirates, and send for friends and relatives in Germany to help them plunder the cities.

1. Note on the sources:

The earliest account of events in the 5th century is that of Gildas, a 6th century monk. Gildas is more concerned with moralising than giving exact information and dates. He sees the fall of lower Britain to the Saxons as a judgement of God on the Britons for their immoral ways, a theme that is echoed by the others. Whilst Gildas writes of 'Saxons', others prefer to use the word 'English'. Bede, writing in 731, uses Gildas for the same period, but supplies dates, and obviously gives an English angle. Nennius' account, of around 800, supplies additional information from other sources, some of which have since been lost. He says that, *he made a heap of all that he found, both from the Annals of the Romans, from the Chronicles of the Holy Fathers, from the writings of the Irish and the English, and out of the tradition of 'our elders'*. Geoffrey of Monmouth bases his History of 1136 on Nennius, but embellishes it with information from unknown sources. However, it is quite possible that he could be drawing on Welsh and Breton tradition and legend.

Booklist:

Sieffre o Fynwy/Geoffrey of Monmouth, by A.O.H. Jarman, Cardiff University of Wales Press, 1966.

The History of the Kings of Britain, by Geoffrey of Monmouth, translated by Lewis Thorpe, Penguin Books, London, 1966.

Wales in History, Book 1 to 1066/*The Invaders*, by David Fraser, University of Wales Press, Cardiff, 1965.

Gildas, the Ruin of Britain, History from the Sources, General Editor John Morris, Phillimore, London & Chichester, 1978.

Nennius, British History and the Welsh Annals, History from the Sources, General Editor John Morris, Phillimore, London & Chichester, 1980.

Arthurian Legends, by Marie Trevelyan, originally pub. in 1895, republished by Parragon, Bristol, 1998.

The Ecclesiastical History of the English People, by Bede, trans. by Leo Sherley-Price, pub by Penguin Classics, 1990.

Chapter 3

The saints came marching in

A new start

Although Christianity had become the official religion of the Roman Empire, it all but disappeared in Britain in the chaos that followed the departure of the legions. However, in Wales, the situation may have been different with it surviving in pockets in the south-east, i.e. in those areas where Roman influence had been strong, such as Aricorum, Blestium (Monmouth) or Caerleon. The Faith was greatly reinforced, if not actually reintroduced by missionaries from Ireland and Gaul who had been inspired by the monastic example of St Martin of Tours. In later years these missionaries and their followers would often be remembered as saints themselves.

However, the descriptions of these missionary/saints and their activities that have come down to us (i.e. in The Lives of Saints) were often written in their present form in the Middle Ages and by then, much in the way of legend had been added to their stories.

St Martin and the saints of Wales

Victory and Decline

No one can serve two masters;
He will hate one and love the other;
He will be loyal to one and despise the other.
You cannot serve both God and money.

Matthew 6;24

By the middle of the 3rd century persecution of Christians in the Roman world was a thing of the past. The Church, now organised with bishops and priests throughout the Empire, had not only won recognition but had become rich and influential in the process. However, by the 4th century, this wealth had corrupted the early vision of personal denial and service to fellow man that the Church leaders had held.

The Monastic Movement. Blessed are the poor.

Go and sell all you have, and give the money to
The Poor, and you will have riches in heaven;
Then come and follow me.

Matthew 19;20

Saint Anthony

By the second half of the 4th century this slide into decadence had provoked a reaction, which in effect amounted to an early Reformation. Devout Christians condemned the Church's wealth and sought a return to the simpler life outlined in the Gospels.

In Egypt, a rich young man, later to become known as St Anthony, renounced his wealth and became a hermit.

Others inspired by his example joined him in a community of monks in the desert where he led them in a life of prayer and fasting. Later when other similar groups were formed, Anthony became their bishop and the Monastic Movement was born.

Saint Martin. Feast day November 11th

In Gaul St Anthony's teachings were taken up by St Martin of Tours. Martin had been discharged from the Roman army as a conscientious objector and had become a hermit on the outskirts of Poitiers. He despised the rich bishops of his day and refused to be like them, preferring rough clothes, simple food and sleeping on a stone floor. Soon his fame as a holy man spread and he attracted disciples. He was so revered that many ordinary people believed him to have the power to raise the dead. In 372AD, against his better judgement, he was persuaded to stand for election as bishop of Tours, and was acclaimed by a huge crowd of voters. However, the established bishops opposed his election, saying that he was *'a lowborn person, of disgusting appearance'*, and as if this wasn't enough, that he was *'shabbily dressed with untidy hair'*.

Unhappy as a bishop Martin returned to the life of a hermit, living at first in a cave some two miles outside the city. Here, he gathered together a monastic school of some eighty pupils, some from noble families. The pupils lived as he did and enjoyed the same simple meals. As well as their daily chores, their days were spent in periods of prayer, study of the classics and transcribing texts. As a result, Martin's pupils were so well trained that they were much sought after and many later became bishops. One such was Amator, later bishop of Auxerre, who is said to have ordained St Patrick of Ireland. As well as establishing his famous school, Martin also travelled the countryside setting up new churches and preaching to the poor, many of whom were strangers to Christianity.

In 383AD the great Magnus Maximus took an army from Wales to conquer Gaul and it is said that he befriended Martin and that when Maximus was eventually defeated and killed, his widow Elen and their two sons took St Martin's message back to Wales. Whatever the truth of this story, missionaries did come to Wales from Gaul and more indirectly, from Ireland, where Patrick had taken Martin's teachings. These missionaries would establish their communities, based on the same principles as Martin's, and later, themselves be remembered as saints. Western Hereford in particular was in the forefront of this Monastic Movement with saints Dyfrig, Beuno and Clodock. In fact Dyfrig (Dyfrig, in Welsh or Dubricus in Latin), was one of the earliest saints of Wales.

Note: Maximus is the Macsen Wledig of Welsh legend to whom Nennius accords the founding of Brittany and the colonising of the land with his Welsh soldiers.

St Dyfrig (Dubricus/Devereux)

Feast day; November 14th

Prince of the Wye

Not only was Dyfrig by far the most important saint in early Hereford but, in the opinion of Canon G.H. Doble, in his *Lives of the Welsh Saints*, also one of the chief figures in the creating of Christian Wales.

He was the illegitimate son of a princess whose story begins around the year 450AD when Pepiau, the king of Ergyng (Archenfield), on returning from a military expedition found that his daughter Ebrdil had become pregnant while he was away. Pepiau was so enraged with the girl that at first, he ordered her to be thrown into the River Wye to drown. But, she kept being washed ashore so he then ordered that she be burnt alive. The next day, when the fire had died out and the king's servants went to inspect the ashes, they found her miraculously sitting on a large stone, nursing a newborn baby. The stone was at Madley (Mat-le = 'a Good-Place' in Welsh), seven miles from Hereford on the old Roman road from Kenchester to Abergavenny. It remains as a memorial to the great man born there.

When the wondrous mother and her boy child were brought to Pepiau, he held the baby in his arms. Pepiau suffered an affliction which meant that he constantly dribbled and there was always dribble on his face, but when the child touched his face, he was instantly cured. The king was so happy that he granted Madley and the tract of land around it to the baby who would be called Dyfrig (from the Welsh *dwfr* = water, possibly because of his association with the Wye*). This area was henceforth to be known as Ynys Ebrdil (Ebrdil's Island), in honour of the boy's mother.

The boy grew up to be very famous. Legend even has it that he was King Arthur's uncle. His fame is attested to by Geoffrey of Monmouth in his *History of the Kings of Britain*, written in 1136AD, where he states that Dyfrig was the Archbishop who crowned King Arthur at Silchester, and that he later became Primate of all Britain and legate of the Papal See. Geoffrey, however, was prone to exaggeration. Dyfrig's 'Life' (as written in the Book of Llandaf) says that he was so famous for his wisdom, scholarship and knowledge of Biblical Law that not only young men, but also older, wiser men and teachers came from all over Britain to learn from him.

There were so many of them that Dyfrig had to establish a monastic college to accommodate over a thousand students, at a place now called Hentland, some four miles west of Ross. The name Hentland itself originates from the Welsh Hen-llan = Old church (enclosure).

Dyfrig and his flock stayed at Hentland for seven years. Then one night an angel appeared in a dream he had. The angel told him to build a new church and settlement back in Ynys Ebrdil at a place near some woodland where he would find a white sow and her young and where the Wye was full of fish. This new settlement would be called *'Mochrhos'*, (Moch-rhos = the Pigs'-heath in Welsh), now called Moccas, about five miles north-west of Madley, on the B4352.

Dyfrig found the place of the white sow and he and his followers stayed there for many years before he retired to Bardsey Island to spend his last days. He is said to have died on the 14th of November in 546AD. However, although like all saints, he had many miracles attributed to him, his real contribution to the Church was his wonderful teaching and great influence on those who followed him. His teaching was said to have shone throughout Britain, 'like a candle on a stand' and it was as a result of his teaching that many of his disciples would themselves become saints and establish their own monastic settlements.

The settlements of the saints

As well as his first church at Madley, then Hentland and Moccas, it seems that Dyfrig and his followers founded as many as twenty-four settlements in what is now

Arthur's cave, Little Doward, Ganarew

The site of Vortigern's castle, Little Doward, Ganarew

Arthur's Stone, near Dorstone, Golden Valley

Venta Silurium (Chapter 1), Caerwent The Capital of Roman Siluria.

The site of Ariconium, near Weston under Penyard.

The Olchon Valley, Ewyas (Chapter 3 Beuno or Chapter 12 Baptists)

Ewyas Lacy Castle, Longtown (Chapter 8)

Hereford Cathedral

The Bishop's Palace, Mathern. Now used as a conference centre.

The church of St Beuno and St Peter, Llanveynoe, in the Olchon Valley (Chapter 3)

Llangorse Lake (Chapter 9)

St Clydog's Church, Clodock

The church at Madley

The church of St Mary and St David, Kilpeck

St Denys, Pencoyd.

Ganarew

St Tewdric's Church, Mathern

St Tewdric's Well, Mathern

St Briavals

St Devereux near the A465

St David's Much Dewchurch

St Dubricius Hentland

Salem, Longtown

The old Market Hall, Ross-on-Wye

Harewood End, A49

The Old House, Hereford

St Briavals Castle

Kentchurch near Pontrilas

The old prisonhouse, Ross

Monnington Court

The Severn Bridge at Beachley. 'The Old Passage' (Chapter 5)

27
ESTD 1872 GWALIA INDEPENDENT STORE ESTD 1872
29

THE COUNTY OF
HEREFORDSHIRE
Welcome to
ENGLAND

HEREFORD
WELSH
SOCIAL CLUB

Pengethley Manor Hotel

MUCH DEWCHURCH

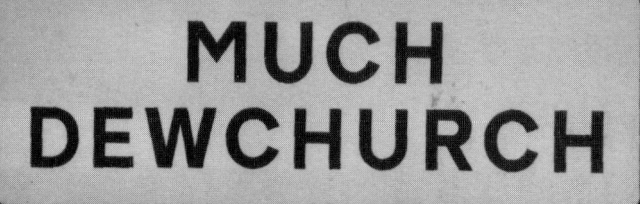

Doward
Biblins

TALYBONT LANE

64

Herefordshire. There were at least three in the Golden Valley*, one at 'Cum Barruc' near Dorstone, at the top end of the valley, another at the lower end of the valley at Abbey Dore and a third at a place called 'Mavurn', the exact location of which is unknown. Sites for some of the other settlements set up by his disciples and clearly identified from old land grants are the modern villages of Ballingham, Dewchurch, St Devereux, Kilpeck, Garway, Pencoyd, Llandinabo, Llanfrother, Llangarran, Llanloudy, Welsh Bicknor and Llancillo.

Outside Hereford, Dyfrig is said to have established several settlements in the Gower peninsular and to have built the abbey on Caldey Island near Tenby so that he and his fellow missionaries would have a retreat away from their teaching and other duties during Lent. Linked to Caldey, he built another monastery at Penally on the mainland opposite the island. Here, another famous Welsh saint, St Teilo, was born.

*Notes:

*In his *Lives of Welsh Saints* Canon Doble sees the location of Hentland as being very significant. He writes, *'The fact that his (Dyfrig's) first foundation was near Ariconium (From which the Celtic kingdom of Erging seems to have got its name) suggests that Ariconium may have been the source of the Welsh Christian movement of the fifth and sixth centuries'*. Although Dubricius/Dyfrig was a native Briton and lived in the rural district of Ergyng, the nearness of the old Roman town of Ariconium and the later tradition that Dyfrig owned land at Caerleon indicate that Welsh Christianity came directly from Romano-British sources.

*The name *'Dore'* in Abbey Dore (Welsh *'dŵr/dwfr'*) means *'water'* and not *'gold'*, for which it was mistaken by the Normans.

*Apparently in Dyfrig's time the Golden Valley was called 'Cum

Cerniu' or in Latin 'Cornubium'. An alternative name for 'Cum Barruc' was 'Llangernwy', perhaps derived from the 'Cornovii', the name of an old Celtic tribe in Shropshire.

The saints of Ewyas

St Clydawg (Clydog or Clodock)
Feast day; November 3rd

If you leave the A465 road from Hereford to Abergavenny at Pandy, just inside the modern Welsh border and follow the narrow, winding lane up the Monnow valley towards Longtown, near where the river Olchon joins the Monnow, you will find the lovely little church of St Clydawg in the tiny village of Cloddock. The saint whose name is honoured was martyred near here in 520AD.

Born in Ewyas in the late 5th century, Clydawg was the son of King Gwynnar of Ewyas and the grandson of King Brychan of Brecon. Brychan had many children and grandchildren and, as most of these became missionaries and saints, it was no surprise that when his father died and he became King, the young Clydawg ruled his kingdom as a devout Christian should. He was said to be ever peace-loving and fair and charitable to his subjects.

Some years after becoming King, he fell in love with the beautiful daughter of a nobleman and she with him. They were soon married but tragically, they did not live happily ever after. Within only a few short weeks of their marriage, possibly on a fine Spring day, Clydawg was out hunting in the woods with some of his nobles when one of them, a jealous rival whose advances his wife had rejected, treacherously killed him with his sword.

Whilst we can only guess at the murderer's fate, we are told that Clydawg's grief- stricken followers placed his body on a cart drawn by two oxen in order to take him home. However, when they came to a ford crossing the River Monnow, the animals' harness broke and the cart became stuck. As there was a small shrine near this spot, those present took it as a sign from God that Clydawg should be buried there. Later, his followers enclosed the shrine and the grave and erected a small church there. They called the place Llan Merthyr Clydawg (The Enclosure of the Martyr Clydawg). In the church was a holy well, the waters of which were said to bring about miraculous cures for all sorts of ailments.

St Beuno
Feast day; April 21st

Leaving Clodock, pass through Longtown and travel up the Olchon Valley until you come to another tiny village called Llanveynoe (or Llan Feuno = The Enclosure of Beuno). Beuno is said to be the son of Hywgi (or Bugi) ap Gwynllyn of Berriw, near Welshpool, in Powys. However, it is possible that Beuno was born in Ewyas.

As a young man he felt drawn to the Church and decided to take Holy Orders at Caerwent, where King Ynyr of Gwent had established a college. Here, Beuno was educated by St Tangusius who taught him about the Holy Scriptures and the Church. After he became a priest, King Ynyr granted him lands in Ewyas, where he set up his 'Llan' (a holy enclosure and monastic settlement). Such was Beuno's dedication and charisma that even the aged King Ynyr became one of his disciples. Beuno's settlement flourished and grew for a period of years. Then he heard that his father was ill and close to death. So, leaving three of his best disciples in charge, he departed for Powys, never to return.

Not long after he arrived in Berriw, his father died, but

not before word of his wonderful sermons had reached the local ruler, who quickly granted him land near the River Severn. A large stone called 'Maen Beuno' (Beuno's Stone) is said to mark the spot where he preached to the people. However, one day he was said to be walking near the Severn when he heard the cries of Saxon huntsmen and the barking of their hounds. Hearing the strange language so alarmed him that, fearing they would invade his lands, he told his monks to pack up their belongings and leave the area with him. From Berriw, Beuno went first to Merioneth and then to Flintshire. From there, in 616AD, he moved again, this time to the Lleyn Peninsula, where he built a great monastery called Clynnog Fawr. He stayed there until his death in 640AD. However, it was in Flintshire that he was said to have performed his most spectacular miracle.

The Tale of Winefride

Winefride (Gwenfrewi in Welsh), the daughter of Thewyth and Beuno's sister Gwenlo, was born in Treffynnon (Holywell) in north-eastern Wales. She grew up to be a beautiful young woman, well known for her kindness and generosity. However, one day, whilst her parents were out attending one of Beuno's sermons in a nearby church, a young prince called Caradoc came to her home and tried to seduce her. Winefride was horrified and ran out of the house in order to seek her parents' protection. Caradoc pursued her and, catching up with her near the church, tried to again to force himself upon her. Screaming, Winefride again resisted and tried to run away for the second time. By now, Caradoc was so frustrated that, in a terrible fit of rage, he pulled out his sword and viciously cut off Winefride's head.

By this time, drawn by the screams, the congregation had come out of the church. Beuno, on seeing what had happened to his niece and Caradoc wiping his bloody sword, called for God's judgement on the killer. With that, the ground opened up and swallowed Caradoc who was never seen again. Beuno then picked up Winefride's head, placed it back on her shoulders and, praying to God, restored her to life. Only a thin scar was left around her neck.

After she was revived, Winefride was so grateful that she vowed to devote the rest of her life to the church and in time she too became a saint. Where her blood had spilled onto the ground a miraculous healing well that is still popular today, sprang forth. That is why the town is called Holywell (holy well). 'Treffynnon', where she was born means 'Town of the Well'.

The Forest of Dean

St Briavel (older Brigomaglos)
Feast day; June 17th

Travelling along the B4228 from Chepstow through the 'Forest' in a northerly direction and just over half way to Coleford you come across the sleepy little village of St Briavels, which is said to be named after an obscure 6th century hermit who founded a church and settlement there. However, scratch a little below the surface and you find Briavel to have really been a much better known person who links the 'Forest' with Cardigan in western Wales, Cornwall and an industrial city in northern Brittany. Briavel is actually St Brioc, one of the 'Seven Founding Saints' of Brittany. His true identity is indeed revealed in the earliest version of St Brioc's *Life*, where the writer also called him 'Briomagl' which changed into 'Briomail' and then 'Briafail' (Welsh 'f' = English 'v'). That Briavel and Brioc's feast days are different is probably due to the variation in name and Medieval writers believing there to be two different men instead of just the one.

St Brioc (Breock, Briuc, Briomaglus)
Feast day; May 1st

St Brioc is described as one of the *'Peregrini'* or wandering holy men who travelled between Wales, Cornwall and Brittany. His *Life* says he was the son of Dingad, grandson of King Brychan, and so cousin to Clydawg, in Ewyas. He was born in Cardigan sometime between 410AD and 440AD and was said to have been educated in Paris as a disciple of the famous St Germanus of Auxerre, along with St Illtud and St Patrick. On his return to Wales, Brioc established several monastic settlements in Cardigan before moving on to found St Briavel's in the Forest of Dean. Then the 'wandering holy man' moved to Cornwall where he established another settlement at St Breocks, near Wadebridge, not far from Bodmin. From here destiny would take him across the sea to Brittany.

At this time the Britons were coming under increasing pressure from the Saxons. The invaders had a firm grip on the south-east of England and, with their armies swelled by reinforcements from Germany, were pressing relentlessly westward. Thus, many of the Britons, in order to escape death or enslavement, fled across the sea to Brittany (Little Britain). This migration was on a large scale and was organised and led by local rulers of the Britons such as Riwal (Hywel), a prince of Dumnonia (south-western England, from which Devon gets its name).

It seems that Brioc was invited by Riwal to join the

emigrants as a spiritual leader and was granted lands by him in order to set up monastic settlements in the prince's new realm in northern Brittany. Riwal, reported by some as being related to King Arthur, is said to have been Brioc's cousin and this has led to speculation that Brioc too was a kinsman of Arthur. Brioc lost no time in spreading the gospel and one of his greatest triumphs came when he converted another Breton ruler, the great Conan, to Christianity.

Today, as well as being remembered as one of the 'Seven Founding Saints of Brittany', he is, because of his great charity to the poor, also remembered as the patron saint of purse makers. His most prominent memorial in Brittany itself is the industrial city of St Briuc in northern Brittany though there are other towns that commemorate him, such as St Briuc des Iffs between St Malo and Rennes and St Briac Sur Mer, to the east of St Malo. He died sometime between 510AD and 530AD.

Booklist:
The Invaders, Wales in History Book 1 to 1066, by David Fraser, (Chap.10, Wales of the Saints), University of Wales Press, Cardiff, 1965.

Lives of Welsh Saints, by G.H. Doble, ed by D. Simon Evans, Cardiff, University of Wales Press, 1971.

The Age of Arthur, A History of the British Isles from 350 to 650, Vol.1 Roman Britain and the Empire of Arthur, by John Morris, Phillimore & Co.Ltd, London & Chichester, 1973.

The Age of Arthur, A History of the British Isles from 350 to 650, Vol.2 The Successor States, by John Morris, Phillimore & Co.Ltd, London &Chichester, 1973.

The History of the Kings of Britain, by Geoffrey of

Monmouth, translated by Lewis Thorpe, Penguin Books, London, 1966.

Lives of the British Saints, by S. Baring-Gould and John Fisher, edited by Derek Bryce, Llanerch Enterprises, 1990.

A Guide to the Saints of Wales and the West Country, by Ray Spencer, pub. by Llanerch Enterprises, 1991.

The Book of Welsh Saints, the age of the saints in Wales, by T.D. Breverton, pub. by Keith Brown & Sons Ltd, Gwasg y Bont, Cowbridge, 2000.

The Oxford Dictionary of Saints, by David Hugh Farmer, Oxford University Press, 1982.

The Celtic Year, A celebration of Celtic Christian saints, sites and festivals, by Shirley Toulson, pub. by Element, Shaftsbury, Dorset.

Chapter 4

Attack and Counter Attack

Juggernaut

The monastic bliss of the sixth century was to be shattered early in the seventh. In the Welsh Annals for the year 516 King Arthur is recorded as having defeated the Saxons at the Battle of Badon, where 'Arthur carried the cross of our Lord Jesus Christ for three days and three nights on his shoulders and the Britons were the victors'.

However, by the middle of the sixth century the Saxons were moving forward again, westwards up the Thames valley overpowering all in their path. In 577, led by their fierce king Ceawlin, they won a great victory over the Britons at Dyrham, near Bristol and captured the cities of Bath, Cirencester and Gloucester. With this victory the Saxons had reached the Severn and separated the Britons of Wales from those of the West Country in Somerset, Devon and Cornwall. There were some setbacks for the Saxons, such as a defeat in 584 when Roger of Wendover records that Ceawlin's army was beaten and routed at a place called Frithenleia, identified by John Rhys as Faddiley on the borders of Cheshire. However, in spite of this, the Saxon advance continued so that by the beginning of the seventh century they had captured much of the lower Severn Valley and were moving into what is now Hereford and the Forest of Dean, sending raiding parties across the Wye. The Book of Llandaf refers to two local kings, Iddon in Gwent and Gwrfoddw in Ergyng, repulsing Saxon attacks in the early seventh century .It also says that at about this time, the northern part of Ergyng was overrun by the Saxons and that monastries founded by Saint Dyfrig had been devastated with the then bishop, Euddogy, and his monks having to flee for their lives, saving what relics, gospels and records that they could. Yet, even now when the Saxon juggernaut seemed unstoppable and the Britons' future looked bleak indeed, an unexpected hero, an old hermit, came forward to save the beleaguered Britons. The story is told in the Book of Llandaf.

The Hermit King

It is written that when he became an old man, Tewdrig, the king of Gwent, retired in favour of his son, Meurig. In total contrast to the hurly burly of being an active ruler of his people, he chose to become a hermit, living among the rocks at Tintern. However, somewhere around the year 620, as he followed a quiet life in his hermit's cell, the Saxons began to invade his son's kingdom in force. Now, because of his fame as a military leader, Tewdrig was persuaded to leave his retreat in order to help his son fight the invaders. The Book of Llandaf says that an angel appeared before him in his meagre little cell and urged him to help his people. The angel is said to have promised victory over the enemy to be followed by a generation of peace. Tewdrig, the patriot, now came out from the hermitage to lead his warriors in a great victory over the Saxons at Tintern Ford, near Brockweir on the Wye, called

'Pont y Saeson' in Welsh i.e. 'the Bridge of the Saxons'. Meurig now pursued the defeated and retreating Saxons before he returned to his father, only to find that Tewdrig had been mortally wounded in the battle. Meurig took his stricken father to Mathern (Merthyr Teyrn = the Martyr King), near modern Chepstow, where he died three days later. A memorial was erected on the spot, which was blessed by bishop Oudoceus, and the land was given to the Church.

Meurig

The victory at Tintern developed into a war during which the Saxons were driven back. Not only was the Saxon advance into south-eastern Wales stopped for far more than the generation promised by Tewdrig's angel, but Meurig also emerged as the strongest leader in the region. Previous to the Saxon invasion, this part of Wales had been divided into several kingdoms in small distinct areas. Now, perhaps because of the Saxon pressure, Meurig came to dominate the whole of south-eastern Wales from the Wye to Gower. But his kingdom was not built on his fame alone. He had also wisely married into the right families. As a young man, he had married into the family of Glywys, the rulers of Glamorgan, and established himself in the Gower area, near Swansea. Later, he married Onbraust, the daughter of Gwrgan Mawr, the king of Ergyng. Gwrgan had no male heirs so Meurig and Onbraust's son, Athrwys, became king on Gwrgan's death. Ergyng now became part of the kingdom of Gwent and the dynasty that Meurig founded was to rule in Glamorgan and Gwent for over three hundred years.

Ithel

One of the Llandaf charters of Ithel ap Morgan, Meurig's great grandson, indicates that those monasteries in northern Ergyng, devastated in Tewdrig's time, were still unoccupied in Ithel's time, possibly because of the continual raid and counter raid along the Wye Frontier. However, in the eighth century the scale of Saxon aggression increased and the raiding turned into attempted invasion. The Chronicle of the Princes reports the Battle of Pencoyd, in 721, which the Welsh won. In 743, there was a massive Saxon attack when king Aethelbald of Mercia and Cuthred of Wessex are reported in the Anglo Saxon Chronicle as having joined forces to fight the Welsh and, although this attack failed, it added to the general ruin of the land.

The devastation is reported as being so extensive that the whole borderland, mainly about the River Wye, but also much beyond, was almost destroyed by the wars and frequent incursions on one side or the other. Many of the monasteries founded by Dyfrig lay desolate and abandoned and the land was swept bare and left unoccupied.

Eventually, in about 745 a peace was negotiated between Ithel and Aethelbald and Ithel now took possession of the abandoned sites and returned them by grant to the Church in the person of bishop Berthwyn. The sites, eleven in all, stretched from Moccas in the north to Llangarron, near Ross, in the east.

Pact

Before joining forces to fight the Welsh in 743, Aethelbald and Cuthred had been fighting each other and had only recently agreed to an uneasy peace. Therefore, the combined attack against the Welsh may have been poorly coordinated, with the two kings falling out with each other again soon afterwards. It is possible that Aethelbald made his peace with the Welsh in order to make war on Wessex. There is also the possibility that as part of their peace agreement Ithel may have promised to help Aethelbald in his war against Cuthred. That Cuthred, after defeating Aethelbald at Burford in 752, then attacks the Welsh in 753, might be some proof of this. Whatever the truth may be, the war between the Saxon kings would be one that Aethelbald would ultimately lose and be killed in battle by Cuthred at a place called Seckington in 755. Aethelbald was succeeded by Beornred who was soon deposed by Offa in 758. Offa would be the greatest of the kings of Mercia and his approach to the Welsh would be unique.

Booklist:
The Welsh Annals, Nennius, Arthurian period sources vol.8. History from the sources, gen. editor John Morris, pub. by Phillimore, 1980.
Roger of Wendover's Flowers of History, 447 to 1066 A.D. Llanerch 1993.
Celtic Britain, John Rhys, 1904 (re-published 1996, Random House).
The Age of Arthur, vol.2, The Successor States, John Morris, Phillimore, 1977.
An Early Welsh Microcosm, Studies in the Llandaf Charters, by Wendy Davies, London, Royal Historical Society, 1978.
The Lives of British Saints, G.H. Doble, ed.by D. Simon Evans, Cardiff,University of Wales Press, 1977.
A History of Gwent, Raymond Howell, Gomer, 1988.

A Guide to the Saints of Wales and the West Country, by Ray Spencer, Llanerch, 1991.
Brut y Tywysogion (or the Chronicle of the Princes), trans. by Thomas Jones, pub. by University of Wales, 1952.

Chapter 5

From Sea to Sea

The mighty Dyke

Since the second half of the seventh century the warlike Mercians had been moving westward, driving the Welsh of the Midlands into the hills beyond The Long Mynd and conquering the fertile lowlands. The Welsh, in turn, struck back in order to regain their lost lands.

Raid and counter raid continued for more than a century then, by the mid eighth century, a new, more aggressive Mercian King, Offa, began to push his conquests even further west. By 784 he had not only captured Shrewsbury itself, but, in order to prevent the Welsh from recapturing their lands, had ordered the building of the great barrier or dyke which still bears the name, Offa's Dyke. However, although the Dyke became the boundary between England and Wales, the bulk of the population in Shropshire and between the Wye and the Severn remained Welsh.

About Offa, the 'magnificent and mighty' King

Offa was the greatest of the kings of Mercia and ruled from 758 to 796. He was formidable to both neighbouring

English kingdoms and the Welsh alike. He already ruled all of the Midlands when he brought Kent and Essex under his control and in 777 he routed the West Saxons, making the Thames the boundary between Mercia and Wessex.

In 789 his daughter, Eadburg, married the king of Wessex. In 792 her sister, Ejfle, married the king of Northumbria. Thus by 792, Offa had greater authority in England than any king before him and exercised control over both Wessex and Northumbria through two dependent kings who were his sons-in-Iaw. That he had friendly relations with Charles the Great of France (Charlemagne) and took the title 'King of the English' further illustrates his power.

Lichfield

Offa wanted to make Mercia the religious as well as the political centre of England and was not satisfied that of the three great kingdoms of Wessex, Northumbria and Mercia, only the latter was without an archbishopric. He made Lichfield a metropolitan see in 786, no doubt hoping that its archbishop would soon be recognised as Primate of all England. However, after Offa's death Lichfield again came under the control of Canterbury.

A bulwark against the Welsh

Wales also felt his might, as Offa consolidated Mercian conquests in the fertile lowlands of the borders and launched attacks deep into Wales in 777 and 783. It was probably because of a Welsh counter attack in 784 that he ordered the construction of the great earthen dyke as an awesome bulwark against any further such attacks. With the Welsh thus contained, he was now free to pursue his expansionist agenda elsewhere. A hundred years later Bishop Asser, in his *Life of Alfred*, wrote that Offa had built a 'barrier from sea to sea' and, although today the Dyke is no longer the boundary between Wales and England, people still use terms such as 'West of Offa's Dyke' to refer to Wales.

Murder most foul. The story of St Ethelbert.

Mighty though Offa was, his reign ended under a very dark cloud. The twelfth century historian Roger of Wendover gives us the most detailed account of the terrible deed. He writes that in 792 (others say 793 or 794), the pious and saintly Ethelbert, king of East Anglia came to ask Offa for his daughter's hand in marriage. Offa, who was at his palace in Sutton Walls, near Hereford, seemed to like the idea of having the king of East Anglia as a son-in-law and so welcomed him in grand style. However, when she was asked her opinion, Offa's wife, Quendritha is said to have advised him to kill Ethelbert and seize his kingdom. Offa is said to have angrily rebuked her, calling her a foolish woman, and saying that such a crime would not only be detestable but would disgrace him and his successors. After his anger had abated Offa went back to Ethelbert and entertained him with feasting, music and dance.

Meanwhile, the wicked queen, still harbouring her murderous intention, had a sumptuous room prepared for Ethelbert. Near the bed was a magnificent chair but under the chair was a pit. At the end of the day when the tired Ethelbert was shown to his room, he was invited to sit down and rest his weary feet. No sooner had he sat down than both he and the chair fell into the pit.

Assassins hired by the queen then leapt out and after stifling Ethelbert's cries with pillows and curtains they killed him.

On hearing what had happened, Ethelbert's friends fled. Offa himself was said to be so shocked that he shut himself in a loft without food for three days. However, regardless of his grief and although, according to Roger he was guiltless, he still sent a great expedition to annex East Anglia to his domains.

The big question in this story is whether or not Offa was involved in Ethelbert's murder. The Anglo Saxon Chronicle has no qualms about blaming him, saying simply that 'Offa king of Mercia commanded Ethelbert's head to be struck off'. Florence of Worcester blames both Offa and his wife, saying that, 'Ethelbert the most glorious and holy king of the East Angles was beheaded by the detestable command of Offa by wicked incitement of his queen'. Offa already ruled Northumbria and Wessex through his sons-in-law, so why not East Anglia? Roger's version might be more accurate. Ethelbert was obviously more concerned with the spiritual rather than real world and would have been easy to control as a son-in-law under Offa's overlordship. Whatever, with the deed done, perhaps by an over-enthusiastic wife, Offa lost no time in annexing poor Ethelbert's kingdom.

As to Ethelbert? He was first buried at Marden then because of his pious nature and the manner of his death, he became regarded as a saint and martyr and his body was reburied in Hereford Cathedral. And Offa? An entry in 'The Chronicle of the Princes' records that he was killed in the Battle of Rhuddlan, near Prestatyn in 796. With his death, his empire also began to die. Even before his death the first Viking raid on Wessex had taken place in 789 and Lindisfarne had been ravaged in 793. But these were only like drops of rain before a storm, a storm that would sweep the kingdom of Mercia away forever.

About the Dyke

What It Looked Like
Offa's Dyke is a large bank of earth with a west facing ditch in front of it, running from Treuddyn, near Wrexham to the Wye at Bridge Sollers, near Hereford and then re-appearing on the lower reach of the Wye. Although over 1200 years of weather, farming, road making and building work have taken their toll, the dyke is still twenty feet or so high in places, especially on the hills. It has been estimated that when it was first erected it was over forty feet in height from the bottom of the ditch to the top. It is possible that at the top there was a wooden palisade running along the dyke with manned outposts at intervals.

The building of the dyke was a massive undertaking, involving many locally recruited construction gangs and an expert team of surveyors. The line of the dyke took full advantage of natural features such as rivers, hills and outcroppings, all with commanding positions looking into Wales.

The Line of the Dyke
As long distance walking becomes more popular, more people get to know about the Offa's Dyke Footpath which runs from Prestatyn in north Wales to Chepstow in the south. Most people assume that the footpath follows the course of the Dyke. This is not so.

Whilst Path and Dyke march together through the central borderland, there is no trace of the Dyke north of

Treuddyn, near Wrexham, although its line was postulated from place name evidence by Sir Cyril Fox, who studied the whole Dyke in great detail in the 1920s and 30s. Again, in the south, Dyke and Path part company on Rushock Hill, near Kington. The Path roughly follows the modern Welsh border south whilst the Dyke takes a south-easterly direction across north Herefordshire, alongside the A480 Kington to Hereford road and reaches the Wye at Bridge Sollers, five miles west of Hereford City. From here to Welsh Bicknor the Wye marked the boundary.

There is a short stretch of the Dyke opposite Welsh Bicknor on the Dean side of the river, then there is a gap where the Dyke could have cut across country to Redbrook, for it is here that it reappears and is rejoined by the Footpath. From here Path and Dyke again progress together along the cliff tops on the English side of the Wye to Sedbury where both make a right angle turn to Sedbury Cliffs thus cutting off the Beachley Peninsula.

Wat's Dyke

The prototype for Offa's Dyke appears to have been Wat's Dyke in the northern borderlands. This great earthwork was probably erected about 720 by king Aethelbald. It stretches from the Severn valley, west of Shrewsbury, near the present border then north to the east of Oswestry where it can be seen near Old Oswestry hillfort before continuing to the Dee estuary, near Holywell. It was built to protect Mercian conquests on the Shropshire plain.

Wat's Dyke runs roughly parallel to Offa's and a few miles to the east of it. However, where Offa's Dyke apparently finishes at Treuddyn, Wat's continues to the coast, giving the impression that in some way, the two dykes complement each other.

Variations in Offa's frontier

When Offa made his boundary he obviously took into account the different natures of the Welsh kingdoms along its length and the different dangers they posed. He must have believed that the greatest threat came in the north. Here, he reinforced Wat's Dyke with a second dyke to the west of it, thus giving an outer line of defence to protect the rich lowlands of Cheshire and Shropshire. The fact that this outer line from Treuddyn to Prestatyn cannot be traced suggests that it may never have been completed by the time Offa was killed fighting the Welsh at Rhuddlan, near Prestatyn in 796.

From the Severn to the Wye at Bridge Sollers, although only a single structure here, the Dyke was a massive forty feet high from top to bottom. This was probably because sometime around 750 Powys had revived under the leadership of king Eliseg, and driven out the English. Offa must have feared that an attack here would not only endanger the newly captured Shrewsbury but also threaten his capital at Tamworth and thus his entire kingdom.

From Bridge Sollers south, was the border with Gwent (including Ergyng and Ewyas). Here Aethelbald had come to an arrangement with Ithel, recognising the Wye as the frontier and it is easy to see why Offa would come to a similar arrangement with Ithel's successors, Gwrgan and Arthwys. Like Aethelbald, Offa was often busy elsewhere, in North Wales, in Wessex and in Northumbria, in addition to consolidating his own diverse kingdom. An amicable agreement with the rulers of Gwent was definitely to his advantage.

Further evidence of such an agreement can be found in the lower reaches of the Wye. Here the Wye presents a clear natural barrier. Yet, without apparant purpose, the

Dyke runs along the top of the cliffs on the English side. However, this part of the river was important to the Welsh for trade such as timber, and the building of the Dyke on top of the cliffs left both banks of the river available for landing by them. More importantly, the Beachly peninsula was left to the Welsh because here was the ferry crossing of the Severn to Aust. This crossing had been used, under the name of the Old Passage, as the direct link between southern Wales and the West Country since prehistoric times. The ferry continued to be used up to the 1960s, when it was superseded by the Severn Bridge.

Booklist:
An Historical Atlas of Wales, From Early to Modern Times, by William Rees, pub. by Faber and Faber, 1972.
Wales in History, Book 1 to 1066, The Invaders, by David Fraser, pub. by University of Wales Press, 1965.
The Anglo Saxon Chronicles, translated and collated by Anne Savage, pub. by Colour Library Books, 1995. For entries 786 Brihtric becomes king of Wessex. 789 Brihtric marries Offa's daughter Eadburg. 789 First Danish ships in Wessex. 794 Raid on Lindisfarne.
Simon of Durham (1129). History of the kings of England, translated by J. Stevenson, 1858, pub. by Llanerch Enterprises 1987. For entries; 790 Ethelred becomes king of Northumbria. 792 Ethelred marries Offa's daughter Elfled. 793 Raid on Lindisfarne.
Roger of Wendover's Flowers of History (1235), translated by J.A. Giles, 1849, pub. by Llanerch, 1993.
Florence of Worcester (1117), a history of the kings of England, trans. by Joseph Stevenson, 1860, pub. by Llanerch, 1990s.

Brut y Tywysogion (or The Chronicle of the Princes, trans. by Thomas Jones, pub. by University of Wales Press, 1952.
Through Welsh Border Country Following Offa's Dyke Path, by Mark Richards, pub. by Thornhill Press, 1976.
Offa: An Eighth Century King and Dyke Builder, pub. by the Offa's Dyke Association, 1991, (pamphlet).
Welshmen, by Thomas Stephens, pub. by J.F. Spriggs/ Western Mail, London/Cardiff, 1901.

Chapter 6

The Overlords

The coming of the Vikings

Towards the end of the 8th. century, new invaders made their appearance in the British Isles. They sailed up the great river estuaries bringing terror from the sea and treating the English much as the English had treated the Britons three hundred years earlier. They were the fierce Northmen, a great seafaring people who came from the coasts of Norway, Sweden and Denmark and were better known as the Vikings. Initially, the Christian countries of western Europe with their rich churches and monasteries were merely places of easy plunder to the Vikings and although their raids continued up to the 11th. century, they soon began to colonise the lands they raided. Thus, by 871, when Alfred became king of Wessex, the Viking Danes ruled most of England. It was because of his success in recovering territory from them that he became a famous and powerful king and earning the title 'Great'.

The ferocity of the Viking raids forced the rulers of Wales into an uneasy peace with their old enemies, the English of Wessex, who, under Alfred, led the Christian fight against the pagan invaders. The new common enemy made it necessary for the Welsh to acknowledge the greater military strength of Wessex by swearing allegiance and paying tribute to Alfred and his successors in return for their protection.

Hywel Dda (the Good)

In 918 one of the Welsh rulers who swore allegiance to Alfred's son, Edward, was Hywel, a minor king from western Wales, who ruled jointly with his brother Clydog. However, Hywel was destined to become a great King, virtual ruler of all Wales who produced a code of laws that was to last for over 600 years, and to be the only Welsh ruler to be called 'The Good'. He would also play an important part in negotiating the 'Wye Frontier' as the eastern boundary of southern Wales.

King of the West

Hywel was of truly noble descent. He was the son of Cadell, son of Rhodri the Great, the most powerful Welsh king of the ninth century who fought both the Vikings and the English and died in battle in 878. Hywel himself had started in a modest way by becoming ruler of what is now Pembroke in 905 when he married the dead king's daughter, Elen.

In 910, on the death of his own father, Cadell, he inherited an equal share of the rest of western Wales together with his brother Clydog. However, in 920, another brother, Meurig, who was probably jealous because he had not been included in the share-out killed Clydog. But, perhaps as a punishment, Meurig did not benefit from his action and Hywel became the sole ruler of all western Wales. Ten years later, in 930, he added Brecon and Radnor to his kingdom.

Friendship with Wessex

Hywel's grandfather, Rhodri the Great, had died fighting the English, but early in his career Hywel decided that it was wiser to pursue a policy of close friendship towards the powerful English kings of Wessex, rather than fight them. He was also ambitious and had his own plans. Thus in 918, together with the other kings of Wales, he gladly swore loyalty to Edward the Elder, and then again in 926, at Hereford, he swore loyalty and paid tribute to Edward's son Athelstan.

His policy of friendship towards Wessex resulted in Hywel being acknowledged as chief king in Wales, both by the other Welsh rulers and by the royal court of Wessex itself where he frequently attended. He was also the first of all the Welsh witnesses to charters concerning Wales from 928 until his death in 950. He demonstrated his power in 937 by keeping the other Welsh rulers loyal to Athelstan when an alliance of Strathclyde Britons, Danes and Scots attacked him at Brunanburgh.

In 942 Hywel's loyalty to Athelstan paid extra dividends when Idwal the king of North Wales turned against the new English king, Edmund, and was killed fighting him. Hywel marched his army north, drove out Idwal's sons and claimed the kingdom for himself. He now directly controlled most of Wales, with the little kingdoms of Glamorgan and Gwent in the south-east readily acknowledging his authority.

The great lawmaker

Hywel admired Alfred the Great and the other great rulers of his time and sought to emulate them in Wales. He minted his own coinage, the earliest by a Welsh king, and even called one of his own sons Edwin after one of king Edward the Elder's sons and, like all great kings, he made a pilgrimage to Rome in 928. Further, like the kings of Wessex he also saw himself as a lawmaker, and so, in 930 he summoned a great gathering of leading church and lay people to Whitland, near Carmarthen, in order to discuss and codify Welsh law and custom. The Code of Laws that resulted became known as the Laws of Hywel Dda and formed the basis of Welsh law down to the Act of Union of England and Wales in 1536.lt was this famous law code, together with the peace and prosperity that his reign brought that earned him the title of 'The Good'.

The Wye Frontier

It was during the meeting at Hereford in 926 that Athelstan, as well as exacting tribute, decreed the river Wye to be the boundary of Wales and soon afterwards he decreed that the river Tamer should be the boundary of Cornwall. There seems to have been some dispute over this boundary, at least according to the chronicler, William of Malmesbury. He says that Athelstan compelled the rulers of Wales to meet him at the city of Hereford and that it was only after some opposition that they agreed to his demands. It is possible that they laid claim to the ancient Welsh boundary of the Severn and the lands between it and the Wye as there would still have been many Welsh people living there. Or, perhaps they thought that the amount of tribute was too high. Hywel was ready enough to pay his share but king Idwal of North Wales was very reluctant to pay. Perhaps Hywel thought the tribute was worth paying because the knowledge that his eastern border was safe from attack and that he had a powerful ally against the hated Danes allowed him to pursue his ambition to unite all of Wales under his rule.

Bishop Cyfeiliog and the great Viking raid

During his reign, Alfred's son, Edward, developed the defensive system of maintaining garrisons in strategically placed towns and cities, some of which he founded himself. These garrisons were highly mobile and could reach trouble spots at short notice. Florence of Worcester, a twelfth century monk, gives us a particularly vivid account of a Viking raid in Ergyng, or 'Yrcenefeld' as he calls it, which clearly demonstrates this system in action.

In 915 two Viking warlords Ohter and Rhoald sailed a large fleet up the Bristol Channel, intent on plunder. They brutally ravaged the Welsh coast and, penetrating inland as far as Ergyng, surprised and captured Cyfeiliog, the bishop of Llandaf, whose see included Ergyng, where he was the 23rd successor to St Dyfrig. Poor old Cyfeiliog was speedily whisked back to the pirate fleet by the triumphant Vikings. However, shortly afterwards, king Edward ransomed him for forty pounds of silver.

Whether Edward thought that he could buy the pirates off with the forty pounds of silver and that this would be the end of the matter or whether he thought he could buy time, we do not know. Whatever, far from being satisfied, the Vikings, perhaps emboldened by this apparent show of weakness by Edward, now landed their whole army and marched toward the plain of Ergyng, no doubt thinking of the rich pickings to be had in the churches there and in the main prize of Hereford, just beyond. But, by now, Edward had managed to mobilise his forces including the garrisons of Hereford and Gloucester, obviously fearing that these were the prime targets. He quickly moved his forces to intercept the raiders somewhere in Ergyng.

In the ensuing battle the Vikings were heavily defeated. Rhoald and Ohter's brother together with many others were killed. Those that survived this initial encounter retreated to an enclosed field where, surrounded, they eventually surrendered, giving hostages as security for their complete withdrawal. However, Edward didn't trust them and so posted sections of his army all along the southern coast of the Bristol Channel from Cornwall to the mouth of the river Avon. True to form, the deceitful Vikings attempted to make night-time raids on the Somerset coast near present day Minehead. However, on both occasions they were met and driven off by the king's army. Utterly defeated, the wretched Vikings now sailed to Flat Holme island, off Penarth, where they stayed until starvation drove them to seek refuge in Dyfed, in western Wales. They stayed there a short while before sailing to Ireland in the autumn.

The ransom
Assuming that Florence's account of the raid is accurate, why would king Edward pay such a large sum of money for a Welsh bishop? Perhaps the answer lies in the political situation in Wales at that time.

When they first asked king Alfred for protection, the little southern kingdoms of Gwent and Glamorgan faced a double threat, one from the Vikings and the other from the aggressive Earl Aethelred of Mercia. However, with the passing of time, this 'protection', which later included all of Wales, in itself developed a strong element of coercion. John Davies, in his *History of Wales*, cites the killing of king Idwal of north Wales when he tried to break free of English patronage as an example. The Hereford meeting with Athelstan, in 926 is another. Therefore it is logical to assume that Edward considered Gwent and Glamorgan (i.e. Cyfeiliog's see of Llandaf), along with the rest of Wales, as his vassals, and so, as overlord, felt duty bound to pay up.

Alternatively, again assuming that Florence is accurate, forty pounds of silver (i.e. 18 kilos) would have been a considerable fortune to pay in ransom then, as it would still be now. Indeed, far too much to pay for a lowly bishop of an unimportant see. It is far more probable that the amount was intended to buy off the Vikings and stop them from attacking Hereford and Gloucester. Cyfeiliog's release may or may not have been part of the deal. It may have merely been co-incidental.

The Ordinance Concerning The Dunsaete

A document known as 'The Ordinance of The Dunsaete' is believed to have originated following the meeting between Athelstan and the kings of Wales at Hereford in 926, where, as well as exacting tribute as overlord, he decreed the river Wye to be the boundary.

The document opens with the statement that it is an agreement that the English Witan and the counsellors of the Welsh have established among the Dunsaete. The agreement first deals with cattle theft across the river before going on to lay down procedures for those Welsh or English who wish to cross or drive cattle into the territory of the other. The document concludes that the Wentsaete formerly belonged to the Dunsaete but that now, more correctly, they belong to the West Saxons (i.e. Wessex) and have to send tribute and hostages there. However, with the king's permission, the Dunsaete should also be allowed hostages for peace. Here the word 'belong' obviously means a vassal acknowledging overlordship.

There are various suggestions regarding the location of the Dunsaete. For example, F. Noble believes that the

Wentsaete corresponds to the later medieval deanery of Archenfield, the old Ergyng, with the Dunsaete corresponding to the deanery of Ross. Another historian, Elizabeth Taylor, sees the Dunsaete as being both sides of the Wye, with Welsh and English being separated by the river. The problem arises because, at the time everyone obviously knew where and what the Dunsaete and Wentsaete were, and the name of the river they were referring to. Most, however, agree that Wentsaete refers to Gwent and that the river is the Wye. Therefore, if the Wentsaete is in fact Gwent, why can't Dunsaete refer to Dean.

Wentsaete = Gwentside (of the Wye)
Dunsaete = Deanside (of the Wye)

If this was the case, the Ordinance would possibly have regulated a stretch of the river separating Gwent and Dean where there was a gap in Offa's Dyke between Welsh Bicknor and Redbrook. Between Redbrook and Chepstow, the steep slopes and cliffs on the Dean side make a cattle crossing unlikely.

The statement that the Wentsaete formerly 'belonged' to the Dunsaete can be taken to mean that prior to 926 the Dunsaete acted as the king's agents in collecting tribute etc., also taking some for themselves. Now, as a result of the new agreement in the ordinance, the Dunsaete could only take hostages with the king's express permission.

Booklist:
Hywel Dda in *Wales in History, Book 1 to 1066, The Invaders*, by David Fraser, University of Wales Press, 1965.
A History of Wales, by John Davies, Penguin Books, 1994.

Wales Before 1066 – a guide by Donald Gregory, Gwasg Carreg Gwalch, 1989.

The History of Wales, a pocket guide, by J. Graham Jones, Cardiff University Press, 1990.

The Kings Before the Norman Conquest, by William of Malmesbury circa 1120, trans. from Latin by Joseph Stephenson, facsimile reprint, LIanerch, 1989.

A History of the Kings of England, by Florence of Worcester, 1141, trans. by Joseph Stevenson, circa 1860, facsimile reprint, LIanerch, 1988.

Wales and England in the tenth century: the context of the Athelstan charters, article by Henry Lloyd, *Welsh History Review Vol.10*, June 1981, University of Wales.

Outlines of British History, part 1, by F.W. Tickner, University of London Press Ltd., 1925.

The Vikings in Britain, H.R. Loyn, B.T. Batsford, London, 1977.

The Archaeology and History of Ancient Dean and the Wye Valley, by Brian Walters, Thornhill Press, Cheltenham, 1992.

Chapter 7

Gruffudd ap Llywelyn and the Borderlands

The warrior king

In 1039, a new and powerful warrior king named Gruffudd ap Llywelyn became ruler of North Wales. His rise to power would be spectacular and his end would be sudden and tragic. However, he would be one of the greatest leaders Wales has ever had. He had two burning ambitions. First and foremost he wanted to unite the whole of Wales under his rule. Secondly, and of more pressing relevance to the borderlands, he wanted secure natural boundaries for his realm, namely, the River Severn (the ancient frontier) and the River Dee.

The battle of Rhyd y Groes

Gruffudd began in the north in the first year of his reign by attacking, and severely defeating Leofric, the Earl of Mercia (the West Midlands) at Rhyd y Groes, near Montgomery. Leofric quickly made peace with Gruffydd and agreed to his seizure of territory west of the River Dee. This land grant was confirmed a few years later by the king of England, Edward the Confessor. It now remained for Gruffydd to conquer southern Wales, and, if possible, to extend his frontier to the River Severn.

In the south his two main adversaries were Hywel ap Edwin in western Wales and Gruffydd ap Rhydderch in southern Wales. By 1044 he had defeated and killed Hywel and the west was his. Gruffydd ap Rhydderch was harder to defeat. He was a popular leader and almost as great a warrior as Gruffydd ap Llywelyn himself. lt took another eleven years to defeat and kill his namesake, the Lord of the South. So, at last, in 1055 Gruffydd ap Llywelyn was master of all Wales and was now able to turn his full attention to the southern borderlands.

King Edward and the Normans

Meanwhile, in England, the Norman Conquest had really began in 1042 when Edward the Confessor became king. Although Edward was the English born son of an English king, Ethelred the Unready, his mother was Norman and he had been brought up in the court of his uncle, Richard the Duke of Normandy. As a result, his background and sympathies were more Norman than English and, naturally, as most of his friends were Norman, he brought them with him and favoured them with positions of power in the church, in his court and throughout his realm. Norman influence made especially rapid progress on the borders of Wales where Ralph, Edward's nephew received lands in Hereford and was made Earl of Hereford in 1051. With him came other Normans, including Osbern Pentecost, who crossed the Wye to build a castle at Ewyas Harold in about 1045, and Richard Scrob who built Richard's Castle near Ludlow. The name 'Harold' in 'Ewyas Harold' was that of Earl Ralph's son, and was given to a later castle built on the same site.

By 1052 a vigorous English resistance to the Normans,

led by the strong Earl Godwin had come to a head. Earl Godwin had played a key part in persuading the Witan (Saxon Parliament) to make Edward king in the first place. Godwin had seen Edward as weak, and had always hoped to control him, but this hope had been thwarted by Edward's Norman friends. Now, in 1052 many of the Normans, including Osbern Pentecost, in Hereford fled. He surrendered his castle at Ewyas Harold and left for Scotland to serve the ill fated king Macbeth. Ralph, the king's nephew, however, stayed in Hereford, even after two severe military setbacks inflicted on him by Gruffudd ap Llywelyn. One was in the same year of 1052, on the 13th anniversary of the battle of Rhyd y Groes, when Gruffudd had invaded and defeated a combined Norman and English army near Leominster. Another followed in 1053, when Gruffudd was again victorious at Westbury. However, Gruffydd, who saw the Normans with their castles as a greater threat than the English, was to inflict an even greater defeat on Earl Ralph.

The Battle of Hereford

Gruffydd had befriended and allied himself to Aelfgar, the son of Leofric, Earl of Mercia, and had married his beautiful daughter Ealdgyth to seal their pact of friendship. In 1055 Aelfgar had fallen fowl of Godwin's sons and had been unjustly outlawed by king Edward in order for them to seize his lands in East Anglia. Aelfgar fled to Ireland where he enlisted a large Viking force of 18 ships. He then sailed to Wales to join forces with Gruffydd who leapt at the opportunity to gain land in the borders. Together, on the 24th of October, the allies marched on Hereford. According to Nina Wedel, in her history of Ewyas Lacy, the route the allies took was along the Golden Valley, taking and destroying the castle at Ewyas Harold in their advance on Hereford. She believes that this route suggests that the Welsh and their allies were focusing their attack on land that had been alienated from them and were avoiding the area of Ewyas to the west of the Golden Valley, which was still firmly under Welsh control.

Earl Ralph, defending the city, led his men some two miles outside to meet the approaching enemies. Contrary to English custom, he insisted that his men be mounted in the Norman fashion. However, at least according to Florence of Worcester, the cowardly Ralph with his Frenchmen and Normans, on seeing the approaching forces of Gruffydd and Aelfgar, is said to have fled the field. The English soldiery, on seeing this, also tried to flee but were unused to being on horseback. What followed was a total rout of the defenders followed by the sacking of Hereford by the victors. One group, probably the pagan Viking Danes, killed seven priests who were defending the cathedral, and then looted and burned it.

The Peace of Billingsley

Edward, on hearing of the sack of Hereford, sent Godwin's son Harold, who had suceeded his father as the strong man of England, with a large army to deal with the invaders. However, these had already left the city, laden with treasure and slaves. Harold is said by Florence of Worcester to have 'entered the Welsh borders, camping beyond Straddle', an old name for the Golden Valley. Having failed to engage the enemy who by now had probably dug themselves into secure positions in the Black Mountains of Ewyas, Harold returned to Hereford which he proceeded to fortify against further attack. In the meantime, messengers crossed to and fro between the opposing armies and a peace meeting between Gruffydd, Aelfgar and Harold was arranged at a place called Billingsley, to the south of Hereford, near Boulston (Bolstone), in Ergyng.

Gruffydd and Aelfgar must have appeared a formidable threat to both king Edward and Harold because, by the Peace of Billingsley, Aelfgar was completely restored to his title and earldom and Gruffydd was allowed to keep all his conquests in the borderlands, including all the lands west of the Wye and large tracts of land between the Wye and the Severn.

Gruffydd swears allegiance

The following year, Gruffydd again defeated an English army. Harold, who was now Earl of Hereford instead of the cowardly Ralph, had made his friend and chaplain, Leofgar, Bishop there. In return, in order to prove his loyalty and devotion to his patron, Leofgar who was more a warrior than a priest, decided to avenge the sack of Hereford by raising an army and attacking Gruffydd. It's possible that he could have been acting on Harold's direct orders but more likely that he acted on his own initiative, knowing that his actions would please Harold. Whatever the reason, his force struck westwards up the Wye valley and met Gruffydd's army at Glasbury, near Hay on Wye where Leofgar and his soldiers were annihilated.

On hearing the news, Harold was shocked and enraged. From then on he came to regard Gruffydd as a greater menace than the Normans and determined then and there to destroy Gruffydd whenever he was able to do so. In the meantime, as a result of Leofgar's aggressive action, Gruffydd was once again threatening Hereford and Edward had to rush to make peace with him. They met at Beachley on the banks of the River Severn, where, in return for keeping the lands he'd conquered, Gruffydd swore allegiance to Edward as his overlord.

Downfall

Harold's hatred of Gruffydd simmered for about six years but as long as Gruffydd and Aelfgar remained friends, he was impotent. When, in 1057, Aelfgar became even more powerful on succeeding his father, Leofric, as Earl of Mercia, Harold again plotted to remove him. In 1058 Aelfgar was again outlawed by king Edward, no doubt on Harold's instigation. However, he was quickly restored with the help of Gruffydd and a Norwegian fleet. Then suddenly, in 1062, Aelfgar died and Harold's enmity knew no bounds as he made his plans for Gruffydd's downfall.

By December he was ready and after Christmas he made his move. With a force of selected horsemen he first made his way to Chester, then made a lightning attack on Gruffydd's headquarters at Rhuddlan. Gruffydd only just managed to escape by sea, to the fury of Harold, who destroyed Gruffydd's castle in his rage. However, Gruffydd's escape was only a temporary respite. Harold's brother, Tostig, invaded North Wales from his earldom of Northumbria, while Harold himself rode south to Bristol where he had prepared an invasion armada with which he patrolled the coastline of Wales, harrying the coastal areas and preventing any Viking help from reaching Gruffydd from Ireland.

Between them Harold and Tostig caused terrible

devastation which was remarked upon over a century later by Gerald of Wales, a 12th. century monk/author. The southern princes abandoned Gruffydd and submitted to Harold and Gruffydd, hard pressed by the relentless brothers, now retreated to the comparative safety of the mountains of Snowdonia. However, by now there were rumblings of discontent even among his own men. Then, on the 5th of August 1063, Gruffydd was struck down by an assassin. Some say that the assassin was Cynan ap Iago, to avenge the death of his father, Iago ap Idwal, alleged to have been killed by Gruffydd in 1039. A more colourful story is that of bishop Madog of Bangor.

Harold, it is said, had put a price of 300 head of cattle on Gruffydd's head. The greedy Madog, who is said to have betrayed Gruffydd's father, Llywelyn ap Seisyllt now arranged the death of Gruffydd. After the deed was done Gruffydd's head was sent to Harold as the price of peace. Harold, though, refused to pay Madog who was now so unpopular that he had to flee the country for his life. He is said to have set sail for Ireland to escape the people's wrath. The ship sank, but only one person was drowned, and that was bishop Madog.

An entry in the Chronicle of the Princes says:

Gruffydd ap Llywelyn was slain, after innumerable victories and taking of spoils and treasures of gold and silver and precious purple raiment, through the treachery of his own men, after his fame and glory had increased, and after he had aforetimes been unconquered, but now was left in the waste valleys, and after he had been head and shield and defender to the Britons.

(translated by Thomas Jones,
University College, Aberystwyth)

Aftermath

Harold's Peace Terms
Following his victory, a jubilant Harold dictated his peace terms to the defeated Welsh. Gruffudd's half brothers Bleddyn and Rhiwallon were to rule in his place as vassals of king Edward the Confessor and to pay tribute to him. Further, the Welsh were to lose much of their territory on the borders. Harold would annex and make part of Wessex all the lowlands between the river Wye and the river Usk, as well as much of Radnor. In North Wales, the fertile lands between the rivers Dee and Conway were to become part of Mercia. Finally, to demonstrate his triumph and to humiliate the Welsh, and also perhaps to bind Mercia to his cause, Harold married Gruffudd's widow, Ealdgyth. She, who had been queen of Wales, would also briefly be queen of England, in that fateful year of 1066.

The South Breaks Away
The first part of Harold's plan for Wales was soon frustrated. With Gruffudd gone, his half brothers could not restore his authority over the south, where new men had seized power. Maredudd ab Owain, a descendent of Hywel Dda lost no time in declaring himself the independent prince of the south-west, with control of the south-east being divided between Cadwgan ap Meurig, in Glamorgan, and Caradog ap Gruffudd, in Gwent. Caradog was the son of Gruffudd ap Rhydderch, killed in battle by king Gruffudd in 1055. Caradog, especially, would have his own views concerning Harold's peace terms.

Archenfield

Meanwhile, of the territories to be annexed, it seems that Harold only got around to occupying two districts, Ergyng, which had seen some of the worst fighting on the border and southern Gwent, near modern Chepstow. For Ergyng, there is a document in the Domesday Book, twenty or so years later, in 1085, listing the rights and duties of the Welshmen of Archenfield (the English name for Ergyng) , which suggests that the war-weary people there came to terms with Harold, pledging their loyalty to Edward the Confessor and promising to serve him in time of war. In return, they were allowed to keep their own Welsh laws and customs. Domesday also shows that they were allowed to continue to pay their rents in the traditional forms of honey and sheep.

The Hunting Lodge

No record exists of a similar submission further west in the annexed territories. However, a reported incident by Florence of Worcester, suggests that Harold was so confident of his control there, that, in 1065, he obviously wanted to show off his conquests to the Confessor, ordered that a large hunting lodge be built at Portskewet a few miles to the west of modern Chepstow. The lodge was to be well stocked with meat and drink, in order that his lord the king might pass some time hunting there.

Caradog, the prince of Gwent, seethed at the loss of parts of his domain and waited for an opportunity to get them back. He had no intention of submitting to Harold and saw the lodge as the symbol of Harold's power in his territory and was determined to destroy it. Thus, on the 24th August, he saw his chance and struck in force, looting and destroying the hated lodge and retaking the district in the process. Most of the men that Harold had left there were killed in the attack. Next, Caradog moved north and east, striking deep into Ergyng. However, Harold was now faced with an even greater crisis further north, and so, never got round to dealing with Caradog.

In the early Autumn, the Northumbrians had finally rebelled against his brother Tostig's violent and despotic rule and had driven him out. In response, Harold assembled an army and marched north to restore peace and re-instate Tostig. But, the Northumbrians refused to have him back and chose instead Morcar, the brother of Edwin, the new earl of Mercia, both of whom were sons of Aelfgar, king Gruffudd's old ally. Rather than face civil war in England, Harold was forced to agree with the bellicose Northumbrians and Tostig was banished, only to return the following year on the side of Harold's enemy, the king of Norway, in an attempt to win his earldom back. The Norwegian invasion failed and Tostig died fighting his brother at Stamford Bridge.

What could have been

The united Wales that Gruffudd had created died with him. Even so, he had restored national pride by raising the power and influence of the Welsh to the highest they had been for centuries and, although his death robbed Wales of its greatest possible defender against the coming tide of the Normans, the pride and sense of nation he had instilled in those who ruled after him served to strengthen Welsh resistance for centuries to come.

On the other hand Godwin and his sons had aggravated the underlying disunity of the great earldoms of England by alienating both Mercia and Northumbria.Their greed had made an enemy of Aelfgar in Mercia, and Harold's obsession with destroying Gruffudd had made him blind to Tostig's excesses in the north.

Matters deteriorated when Harold was forced to agree to Morcar becoming earl of Northumbria. Now the two great northern earldoms were ruled by two brothers who hated the Godwins and their House of Wessex. Harold also made a deadly enemy of his own brother Tostig in the process. Moreover, there was still fighting in the Welsh borderlands.

Rather than use brute force to try to solve all his problems, Harold could have made a powerful ally in Gruffudd ap Llywelyn and with his help and influence in Mercia, could have checked the forces of disintegration in England. With such an ally, it is possible that Harold and Anglo Saxon England could have survived the coming storm of invasion in 1066, instead of being swept away by it.

Raids across the southern Wye into Dean

Although Gruffudd ap Llywelyn gets most of the limelight throughout this period, his rival and namesake in the south also made several large scale incursions into Saxon held borderlands before his death in battle against the northern Gruffudd in 1055.

In 1049, the southern Gruffudd's kingdom had been faced with an invasion of Danes from Ireland. His response had been twofold. First he moved everything of value to inland woods, out of reach of the invaders. Next, he sent envoys to negotiate with the invaders in order to make a common cause with them and divert them from his shores to those of his neighbours in south-eastern Wales and The Forest of Dean. Although, at this time south-eastern Wales was ruled by Meurig ap Hywel and his son Cadwgan of the ancient House of Morgannwg, Gruffudd had family links with Gwent and Ergyng and saw an opportunity, in alliance with the Vikings, to extend his rule eastwards.

Therefore, in August of the same year, 1049, Gruffudd led the combined forces of Danes and Welsh in a fleet of 36 Viking ships to the mouth of the Usk. And when they had finished looting and ravaging there, he led the raiders across the Wye to attack the great manor of Tidenham which was also ravaged without mercy.

Bishop Aldred of Worcester called up the shire forces of Herefordshire and Gloucestershire in order to counter the invasion but the response to his call was poor. Further, the border Welsh, some of whom had been conscripted into his force were so discontented with their Saxon masters that they sent a messenger to king Gruffudd requesting him to come to their assistance and attack the English as soon as possible. Thus, at daybreak on a summer's morning, Gruffudd and his Viking allies made a surprise attack on the English camp and scattered with great slaughter the force intended to stop him. J.E. Lloyd, in his *History of Wales*, remarks that this victory was turned to good account by the southern king in the next few years. For now, the Forest of Dean was his.

Booklist:
Florence of Worcester, A History of the Kings of England, 450AD to 1141AD facsimile reprint, Llanerch Enterprises.
History of England and Wales, from the earliest times to 1485, by Howell T. Evans, The Educational Publishing Co.Ltd., Trade Street, Cardiff, 1908.
Wales in History, Book 1, The Invaders, by David Fraser,

University of Wales Press, Cardiff, 1965.

Ewyas Lacy and the Origin of Longtown, by Nina Wedel, 1998, pub. by the author, Crown Cottage, Longtown, Herefordshire, HR2 OLS.

Brut y Tywysogyon or The Chronicle of the Princes, Peniarth MS. 20 version, translated with introduction by Thomas Jones, University of Wales Pess, 1952.

Welshmen, a sketch of their history, from the earliest times to the death of Llywelyn, the last Welsh prince, by Thomas Stephens, Western Mail, Cardiff, 1901. For the story of bishop Madog killing Gruffudd.

A History of Wales, by John Davies, Penguin Books, London, 1990, ref. to Ulster Chronicle entry concerning Cynan ap Iago killing Gruffudd.

A History of Wales, vol.2, by John Edward Lloyd, Longmans, Green & Co, London, 1911.

Chapter 8

The Lords of the March

The conquest of Wales

Within months of the Battle of Hastings most of England was firmly under King William's control. The hated timber castles of the Normans on their mounds of earth sprouted up everywhere and within a few years, even the last desperate attempt to oust the invaders, led by Hereward the Wake in 1071, had failed. Wales, however, was not so easily conquered. Here the conquest took centuries and created a unique frontier territory known as The March of Wales.

The plan for Wales

The Border Sentinels

The stiff resistance met by the Normans in the borderlands of Wales led them to adopt a different strategy to that used for England. William first needed to secure his western frontier from attack by the Welsh who could be very dangerous under an able leader such as Gruffudd ap Llywelyn. In order to do this, he appointed some of his most able lieutenants as earls of the great border strongholds of Hereford, Shrewsbury and Chester. From these bases not only would they defend the frontier, but also make forays across the frontier into Wales itself. In Hereford, William made his kinsman, William Fitzosbern earl in 1067.

The creation of the March

The second part of William's strategy was to encourage his followers to invade and conquer Wales piecemeal by giving them a free hand to use their own private armies to seize Welsh territory. In return they would enjoy power undreamed of by their counterparts in England. Wales became a land of great opportunity where, apart from acknowledging the over-lordship of the king of England, these Norman adventurers could rule their conquests like petty kings. Just like kings they had their own laws, the Laws of the March, mentioned in Magna Carta and often based on the old Welsh laws of Hywel.

As well as making war on the Welsh they could even, again like kings, make war on each other, in order to settle disputes. The lordships they ruled were often based on older Welsh units of government such as cantrefs (hundreds) and commotes, where the Norman lord simply replaced the native Welsh ruler. A.D. Carr, in his book on Medieval Wales, says that 'for many Welshmen, then, the coming of the Normans meant a change of ruler, although they did not come under the authority of the English crown; their new lords owed homage to the king but they were at the same time, independent rulers and very jealous of their independence'. Thus Clifford, listed in the Domesday Book as being in the hands of one Ralph of Todeny, brother in law of Fitzosbern, was virtually a sovereign state.

Consequently, as a result of the Norman invasion, Wales became divided into two areas. The first was still ruled by native Welsh princes and known as 'Wales proper' or *pura Wallia*, the second was ruled by semi-independent Norman lords. It lay between England and Wales proper and was called the 'March of Wales' or *marchia Wallia*. Marcher Wales was not part of the kingdom of England. It was a frontier zone, created by the Norman advance into Wales but it was to last beyond the conquest of Wales in 1282 and well into the 16th. century.

Fitzosbern and the De Lacys

The condition of the borderlands
As a result of the border wars along the Wye between the Welsh and the Saxons before 1066, much of Straddle (the Golden Valley) and northern Ergyng are recorded as sparsely inhabited wasteland in the Domesday Book in 1086. The desolation was compounded between the years 1067 and 1070 by the activities of a Saxon rebel from Shropshire called Edric the Wild. Edric, with the help of the Welsh kings Bleddyn and Rhiwallon, invaded and devastated north Hereford as far as the river Lugg. Bleddyn and Rhiwallon no doubt saw an opportunity to regain the borderlands that their half brother Gruffudd ap Llywelyn had recaptured during his reign. However, in spite of the ferocity of the attack, the Norman garrisons in their timber castles stood firm and Edric and his allies appear to have been driven back. However, two years later in 1069, they still had sufficient strength to attack and burn Shrewsbury, laying siege on the garrison there. Fitzosbern now acted with speed and dispatched his forces from Hereford to relieve the situation. Edric was defeated and he eventually made his submission to king William in the summer of 1070.

William Fitzosbern

Back in Hereford, in spite of Edric's rebellion, Fitzosbern made rapid progress in his task of securing the borderlands. During the few years from 1067 until his death in 1071, he rebuilt the castle at Ewyas Harold and built new castles at Wigmore, Clifford, Monmouth and Chepstow. These castles not only marked and protected his frontier, as king William had primarily wanted, but also acted as bases for further attacks on the Welsh. From these bases Fitzosbern advanced westward to Brecon where he defeated Cadwgan ap Meurig, the king of Glamorgan. Further south he advanced along the old Roman road from Chepstow to the ancient Roman headquarters of Caerleon where he built yet another castle.

Perhaps because of the depopulation caused by the border wars, Fitzosbern did not attempt to displace the Welsh population in areas he had occupied. Rather than demand complete subjugation and displacement of the local people, he appears to have followed a consistent policy of accommodation and absorption. So, when he annexed Archenfield, the old kingdom of Ergyng, he honoured an agreement that its Welsh inhabitants had made with Edward the Confessor, following king Gruffudd's defeat. By submitting to Norman rule, and pledging their support and allegiance to their new masters, they were allowed to keep their customs intact.

Walter de Lacy

One of Fitzosbern's most faithful followers, who had been with him on his expedition into Brecon, was Walter de Lacy, from Lassy in Normandy. For his services to king William and Fitzosbern, Walter had been granted extensive estates in the borderlands. In 1074 Walter helped bishop Wulfstan of Worcester to suppress a rebellion against the king by the new Earl of Hereford, Fitzosbern's son, Roger de Breteuil, together with Ralph Guander, Earl of Norfolk. For his part in the rebellion, Roger was jailed for life and his lands confiscated. Ralph fled to Brittany. The grateful king William then further rewarded Walter with some of the confiscated Fitzosbern lands, including the small Welsh commote of Ewyas seized from the kingdom of Gwent by Fitzosbern.

Roger de Lacy

Walter de Lacy was killed in an accident, in 1085. He was succeeded by his son Roger who took control of the sparsely populated commote in the Black Mountains. The commote was to the west of land he already held near Ewyas Harold. However, the extent of his control is not made clear in the Domesday Book, which records that he was to receive a typically Welsh yearly rent of fifteen 'sesters' of honey (about 60 lbs or 27 kilos) and fifteen pigs from the locals. He also had the right to hold court and dispense justice, this last being qualified by the phrase *'when the men are there'*, a phrase which Lynn H. Nelson in his book on the Normans in southern Wales, believes may refer to the semi nomadic customs of free tribesmen.

Although manpower in the borders was scarce, Roger for his part, like Fitzosbern, made no attempt to displace the native Welsh. He seems to have been content with the revenue and the power he exerted in his role as virtual prince in the commote. For the locals, apart from a new lord and the new name of Ewyas Lacy, little had changed. They paid the same rents as they had always done, took their complaints to their local ruler as they had always done and generally carried on with their lives in the same way as before.

Roger and the King

Unlike his father, Roger wasn't a loyal kingsman. In 1088, he, just like his namesake fourteen years earlier, became involved in a plot against the king. William II, called 'Rufus' because of his red face, had succeeded his father in 1087, instead of his older brother Robert, who became Duke of Normandy. Rufus was unpopular with many of his barons because, like his father before him, he sought to curb their powers. Also, the barons wanted to see England and Normandy united under one ruler again and they believed that Robert as that ruler would allow them greater freedom of action. Consequently, just after Easter 1088, under the leadership of Rufus' own uncle Odo of Bayeux, the rebel barons struck. The war was described by Florence of Worcester as worse than civil war, where fathers fought sons, brothers fought brothers and friends fought friends.

Roger, together with Ralph de Mortimer of Wigmore, joined the uprising. First they seized Hereford, then, with other Marcher lords, including Bernard de Neufmarche, and along with men from Hereford, Shropshire, and Wales, they marched on Worcester. There, although they ravaged the countryside, they failed to take the city, which was defended by the same loyal bishop Wulfstan who had suppressed the rebellion in 1074. Wulfstan not only repelled the rebels, but defeated them with a great slaughter and captured many prisoners. Roger was lucky in that he shared in a general amnesty that Rufus, no doubt because of the extent of the rebellion, had granted to the principal rebels.

However, in 1095, Roger foolishly became involved in another conspiracy led by Robert de Mowbray, the Earl of Northumberland. This time there was no amnesty for him and for his part in this plot, Roger was banished and all his possessions were given to his brother Hugh.

It was Hugh de Lacy who in 1108 gave lands for the founding of Llanthony Priory in the Honddu valley. However, when he died in about 1118 without male heirs, king Henry I, the Conqueror's youngest son, granted part of his estates to the lord of Ewyas Harold, Payn Fitzjohn, who was married to Hugh's daughter Sybil. Payn became sheriff of Hereford and Shropshire. He was killed repelling a Welsh attack in 1137. The part of Hugh's estates, which included Ewyas Lacy was granted to Joce de Dinan, who supported Henry I's daughter Matilda in the ruinous civil war, called 'The Anarchy', in which Matilda fought her rival Stephen for the throne. These lands were recovered by Hugh's nephew Gilbert in about 1153, at the end of this civil war, when king Stephen and Matilda reached an agreement at Wallingford.

The nature of Norman settlement

Although often judged as harsh and oppressive as rulers, the Normans, unlike the Anglo Saxons, in the early years of their conquest of England neither enslaved nor displaced the native populations they found in the lands they conquered. The Anglo Saxons came as land hungry colonists, taking the land for themselves. The Normans came seeking power and wealth as rulers and made full use of whatever human resources they found in an area. Thus, in the Marches they often simply took the place of a local lord or princeling and like local lords, they also married into other landed families, be these Norman or Welsh. A century earlier, the Normans had been Viking Northmen but they had adopted French ways. In England, they became the Anglo-Norman ruling class, in Wales they became Cambro-Norman lords and in Ireland they became Norman Irish with names like Fitzpatrick still common.

There are many examples of diplomatic marriages in the March of Wales. Gerald the Welshman, whose books give a contemporary insight into 12th. century Wales, described himself as being sprung from the princes of Wales and the barons of the Marches. However, being married to the daughter of his Norman neighbour Picot de Sai, did not stop Cadwgan ap Bleddyn from driving the Normans back to Chester in 1094. Another and perhaps the most ironic example of a Cambro Norman marriage in the Marches, is that of Nest, the daughter of king Gruffudd ap Llywelyn, *'Terror of the Border'*. She married Osbern Fitz-Richard, the son of Richard Fitz-Scrob of Richards Castle in north Herefordshire. Fitz-Richard and Nest had a daughter, Agnes, who married Bernard de Neufmarche who was involved in the rebellion of 1088 and later invaded and seized control of Brecon. And so, the line of the Warrior King joined that of his enemies, The Lords of the March.

Booklist:
Land of my Fathers, by Gwynfor Evans, John Penry Press, Swansea, 1974.
History of Wales, Vol.II, Conquest and co-existence and change, Wales 1063 to 1415, by R.R. Davies, University of Wales Press, 1987.
Medieval Wales, by A.D. Carr, chapter 2, 'The Norman Challenge', 'The Making of The March', Macmillan Press, 1995.
Wales Through the Ages, Vol.1, Ed. by A.J. Roderick, Chapter on The Norman Conquest, by William Rees; The Welsh Awakening, by I.Ll. Foster; The Wales of Gerald, by

Thomas Jones, pub. by Christopher Davies Ltd. Llandybie, Carmarthen, 1959.

The Normans in South Wales 1070-1171, by Lynn H. Nelson, pub. by University of Texas Press, Austin and London, 1966.

Ewyas Lacy and the Origin of Longtown, by Nina Wedell, pub. by the author, Crown Cottage, Longtown, Herefordshire, 1998.

Florence of Worcester, a history of the kings of England (450 to 1141), translated by Joseph Stevenson c.1860, facsimile reprint by Llanerch Enterprises.

History of England and Wales, From earliest times to 1485, by Howell T. Evans, M.A., The Educational Publishing Co.Ltd., Cardiff, 1908.

Chapter 9

The Twelfth Century

A battle for body and soul

With the rebellion and downfall of Fitzosbern's son Roger de Breteuil, Earl of Hereford, in 1074, the Norman advance in southern Wales faltered. Welsh resistance stiffened under the leadership of Rhys ap Tewdwr, prince of southern Wales, a descendent of Hywel Dda, but Rhys was killed in battle when Bernard de Neufmarche invaded and conquered Brecon in 1093. Later, during the Anarchy of Stephen and Matilda, the Welsh regained much of their land. And so the pendulum would swing, first to the Normans, then to the Welsh up until the death of Lywelyn the Last in 1282.

However, whilst the battle for the land of Wales was going on, so too was another battle, the battle for the soul of the country. The Normans sought to bring the Welsh church under the control of Canterbury. They started taking over the church in 1107 when Urban, a Norman, became bishop of Llandaf.

He was the first of the bishops in Wales to swear allegiance to Canterbury. He was followed in 1115, when, with the pope's backing another Norman, Bernard, was appointed as bishop of St David's. He too acknowledged the supremacy of Canterbury although he would have his own ambitions concerning St David's.

Urban, Bishop of Llandaf

A reforming bishop
Urban was bishop of Llandaf from 1107 to 1134. He welcomed the link with Canterbury, as he probably believed that he needed a powerful patron to help him keep church property out of the hands of greedy Norman knights. He had grand ideas for his church. At his appointment he set about re-organising the old Celtic church on typical Latin lines, appointing deans and creating small parishes. Then, in 1115, he began rebuilding the church at Llandaf itself so that he would have a cathedral worthy of his diocese. Some of his work can still be seen there, along with other examples of the Romanesque style he favoured at churches at Chepstow and Ewenni, near Bridgend. It was his attempt at re-organisation that caused him his greatest problems.

The Organisation of the Old Celtic Church
The old Celtic Church of Wales had been developed in the Age of Saints and most of the saints had started out as hermits, moving from place to place preaching the Good News. On their travels these saints made friends and disciples and often settled with them for a time. They would also be given grants of land by local kings so that they could establish monastic communities. Such communities would be called 'clasau', with a chief monk or abbot in charge of each 'clas'. Sometimes this would be the saint himself before he moved on to found a new community elsewhere. Saints would leave in their wake a series of churches dedicated to them. The result would be that in time the saint or his successor might have a number of such dedicated monasteries and churches

under his spiritual control and so be recognised as a bishop.

However, unlike the twelfth century Norman concept of a diocese where one bishop controlled all the churches in a given area, in the Celtic Church different bishops might control churches intermixed in the same area. Thus, when a Norman bishop such as Urban sought to re-organise his diocese along Roman lines, there were often areas in dispute. In south-eastern Wales such areas were Ergyng/Archenfield and Ewyas which Urban claimed for Llandaf but which were also claimed by St David's and Hereford dioceses.

Urban's Arguments

Urban used two arguments. Firstly, he claimed that the diocese of Llandaf was based on the old kingdom of Glamorgan and that this kingdom had, at various times in the past, not only included Gwent and the border lands west of the river Wye but also a part of Brecon and large tracts in western Wales up to the river Tywi. His second argument was that he claimed jurisdiction over all the churches dedicated to the three patron saints of Llandaf namely Dyfrig, Teilo and Euddogwy. To strengthen this particular argument he commissioned the compilation of the Book of Llandaf from which we get many of the stories about the Saints of Wales, not to mention the details of land grants made to these saints.

The Book of Llandaf

The Book of Llandaf, or the *Liber Landavensis*, consists of a large collection of biographies of saints, copies of surviving charters and land-grants and contemporary twelfth century records such as papal bulls, letters and lists. The book is a veritable treasure house for anyone interested in the early history of south-eastern Wales.

It was probably compiled by monks at Llancarfan in the Vale of Glamorgan in around 1125 in order to prove that Llandaf had been a diocese rich in property and extensive in area for at least 600 years. However, although the book appears to document the history of the diocese from the late fifth century to the eleventh, the non-diocesan nature of the old Celtic Church calls this into question. Consequently the book's compilers have been accused of faking evidence in order to further the ambitions of Urban and Llandaf.

However, in spite of these doubts, Wendy Davies who has studied the Llandaf charters and land grants believes that much of the documentation in the book was copied from earlier material, and that, although the book's compilation could have been manipulated to suit Urban's claims, this earlier material was substantially genuine, thus making *Liber Landavensis* a valuable source for historical investigation.

Similarly, although the saints' lives were embellished with miraculous events to increase their importance and links with Llandaf exaggerated where necessary, the biographies themselves were not purely twelfth century fiction, but were, in fact, based on earlier lives, stories and legends. For example, the story of Tewdric defending the river Wye at Tintern is dramatically exaggerated by having angels rather than a human telling him of the Saxon invasion. Consequently his death as a result of the following battle becomes a martyrdom.

Urban's Enemies

In making his claims, Urban aroused the enmity of both the bishops of Hereford and St David's. Hereford claimed that, since Archenfield was now administered by the Earl of Hereford, it should be part of its diocese as well. The claim of bishop Bernard of St David's, who stood to lose much of his diocesan territory, was different. He said that Saint David had been Archbishop of all of Wales and he now demanded that his diocese should be elevated to an archbishopric once again, with authority over the other Welsh dioceses and with him as the archbishop. Further, as there were churches dedicated to St David throughout southern Wales, including some in Archenfield, Bernard said his claim took precedence over that of Llandaf.

The letters and papal bulls in the Book of Llandaf refer to Urban's bid to increase his diocese and indicate that by 1129 he'd won much of what he claimed, at least as far as the eastern districts of Archenfield and Ewyas were concerned. However, when he was on his way to Rome in 1134, possibly to further press his claims on areas in western Wales, he suddenly died. When they heard the news, the bishops of Hereford and St David's pounced with their own claims. The matter was eventually settled with Llandaf losing most of what it had claimed. Archenfield was lost to both Llandaf and St David's, becoming a deanary of the diocese of Hereford, and Ewyas became part of St David's where it remained until 1852.

Gerald the Welshman

In 1188 Archbishop Baldwin of Canterbury undertook a tour of Wales in order to recruit fighting men for the third Crusade. Baldwin's right hand man on this journey was the Archdeacon of Brecon, Gerald de Barri, famous for the book he wrote about this journey and better known as

Giraldus Cambrensis or Gerald the Welshman. Whereas Urban, on the one hand, was instrumental in producing a book which has turned out to be a mine of historical information concerning the early history of south-eastern Wales, Gerald, on the other hand, wrote a stunningly detailed contemporary account of twelfth century Wales, including specific references to the southern borderlands.

Gerald was a typical Cambro-Norman, the son of a Norman knight, William de Barri, so named after Barry Island, in Glamorgan, which Gerald tells us had been named after a sixth century saint, Saint Barruc. His mother, Angharad, was the half Welsh, half Norman daughter of Nest, the daughter of the same Rhys ap Tewdwr who was killed defending Brecon against Bernard de Neufmarche in 1093. Gerald's father's brothers had been called 'the sons of Nest' and had been in the forefront of the Norman invasion of Ireland, and he himself had been to Ireland and written two books about it.

Gerald wrote extensively in Latin. However, although he wrote at least seventeen books altogether, he is famous in Wales for two in particular, namely *The Journey Through Wales*, and *The Description of Wales*, both of which had several editions from the 1190s to 1215. His 'Journey' describes, in diary like detail, his travels with Archbishop Baldwin and, as well as giving vivid descriptions of the Wales he knew so well, it also includes his comments on places and people, together with many stories of the places he was travelling through. His 'Description' reads like a digest of facts and figures which, as well as describing Wales, gives his opinions on what he saw as the good and bad points of the Welsh people, how they could best be conquered and how the Welsh could best resist being conquered. Both books supply invaluable contemporary information for any historian. The following are extracts from these two books relevant to the southern borderlands.

Llanthony

Gerald must have been very fond of the monastery at Llanthony which he describes in glowing words. He writes of it as being shut in on all sides by a circle of lofty mountains and says that the site is the most suited to the practice of religion in the 'whole Island of Britain'. The monks could sit in their cloisters in this monastery, breathe the fresh air, gaze up at distant views rising above their own high rooftops, and see, as far as any eye could reach, mountain peaks which rose to meet the sky and often, herds of wild deer in the distance.

The monastery was originally founded by two hermits so that they could live in solitude away from the bustle of everyday life. It was built on the bank of the Honddu river from which it takes its name, Llanhonddu. In Welsh, it had originally been Llanddewi Nant Honddu i.e. The church of David on the Honddu brook. Llanhonddu has been corrupted to Llanthony in English.

The two original monks, William, a former knight, and Ernisius, a priest, had followed the vows of poverty of St Benedict, believing that as the Church of Christ increased in riches so it decreased in virtue. Later, these two became distressed when their church became endowed with land and wealth, first by Hugh de Lacy, its original lord and then by other faithful benefactors. As the church became wealthy, later monks adopted the less strict rule of Augustine. However, the Augustines' way of life was probably closer to the original Celtic monastism and 'clas' of the old Welsh Church. Many of the 'clasau' in Wales adopted it when changing from Celtic to Latin Christianity.

The see of Llandaf

By Gerald's time the Normans had a strong grip on the Welsh Church and in part, Bishop Baldwin's tour had been intended to reinforce this grip. However, Gerald believed, like Bernard earlier in the century, that the diocese of St David's had once been the Metropolitan See of Wales and it was his burning ambition to restore it as such, with him as Archbishop of Wales. Gerald was to be disappointed in this when in 1176, his uncle David Fitzgerald, the bishop of St David's died, and he was passed over by king Henry II in favour of an obedient Norman, Peter de Leia, instead. Henry made it plain that he did not want another bishop with royal Welsh blood in his veins at St David's.

In chapter 4 of *The Description of Wales* Gerald makes it plain that he believed Ergyng to have once been in St David's diocese. He says of St David's that it once had twenty-four cantrefs but that in his day it only had twenty-three, with Ergyng, called Archenfield in English, then being in the diocese of Llandaf. This is an interesting point because if Gerald is right this would mean that Ergyng was still in Llandaf in 1215 when the second edition of *The Description* came out. Ewyas was to remain in the diocese of St David's until 1852.

The Border

The old boundary between southern England and Wales writes Gerald, was the Severn, which rises in the Plynlimon Mountains, flows around Shrewsbury Castle by Bridgenorth Castle, on through the city of Worcester, then through Gloucester to flow into the Severn Sea. He says it is named 'Hafren' in Welsh after the daughter of Locrinus who was drowned there. The Romans changed the 'H' to an 'S' to give 'Severn', just as they changed Greek HEMI into Latin SEMI.

As regards the southern border, in spite of Archenfield being administered by Hereford when he wrote his *Description of Wales*, Gerald clearly places it in Wales. The Wye, he writes, rises in the same Plynlimon Mountains and flows by the castles of Hay, Clifford and on through the city of Hereford. Next it passes Wilton and Goodrich castles, goes through the Forest of Dean, which is full of deer and where iron is mined, and then enters the sea near Striguil (Chepstow) Castle. The Wye, he continues, forms the 'modern' boundary between England and Wales.

The Power of the Marcher Lords

One of the stories Gerald told was about his own great uncle, Gruffudd, the son of Rhys ap Tewdwr, the prince of southern Wales. It is a dig at Norman power.

One day in Winter, in the reign of Henry I, Gruffudd was riding past Llangorse Lake, near Brecon. He was in the company of Milo, Earl of Hereford and Lord of Brecon and Payn Fitz John, the Lord of Ewyas. Earl Milo was making fun at Gruffudd's expense. He said that there was an old story locally, in Wales, that if the rightful ruler of the land came to this lake, which was covered in waterfowl of various kinds, and ordered the birds to sing, they would burst into song. Gruffudd answered by saying that since Milo ruled the country he'd better be the first to speak to the birds. The waterfowl took no notice of

Milo. Then Payn spoke to them but again they took no notice. Now, at last, it was Gruffudd's turn. He got off his horse, knelt down facing east and fell forward, face to the ground and lay flat. Then, he raised his eyes and hands to heaven and prayed to God. When his prayer was finished he stood up, made the sign of the cross and said, 'Almighty God, Jesus Christ our Lord, show Your miraculous power to us here today. If You have ordained that I should descend in direct line from the five princes of Wales, make these birds declare it in Your name'. Immediately, all the birds on the water beat their wings and began to sing to proclaim him master. Everyone present was astonished.

Milo and Payn Fitz John hurried back to the king's court to tell him what had happened. King Henry replied that he wasn't surprised and went on to say that it was they, the Normans, who held power and so were free to commit acts of violence and injustice against the Welsh people, while knowing full well that the Welsh were the rightful heirs to the land.

Booklist:
Wales in History, Book 1 to 1066, The Invaders, chapter 10, Wales of the Saints, by David Fraser, Uni. of Wales Press, Cardiff, 1965.
Wales in History, Book 2, 1066 to 1485, The Defenders, chap.4, Gerald of Wales, by David Fraser, Uni. Wales Press, Cardiff, 1967.
A History of Wales, by John Davies, Penguin Books, 1994, chapter 4.
An Early Welsh Microcosm, studies in the Llandaf Charters, by Wendy Davies, London Royal Historical Society, 1978.
The Kings before the Norman Conquest, by William of

Malmesbury (12th century), translated from Latin by Joseph Stephenson, reprint by Llanerch Enterprises, 1989.
The Age of Conquest; Wales 1063-1415, by R.R. Davies, pub. Oxford Uni. Press 1991, (chap.7, Church and religion in an age of change).
Lives of the British Saints, by S. Baring Gould and John Fisher, edited by Derek Bryce, Llanerch Enterprises, 1990, (introductory remarks concerning twelfth century written saints' lives).
Gerald of Wales, The Journey Through Wales/The Description of Wales, translated with an introduction by Lewis Thorpe, pub. Penguin Books, London, 1978.

Chapter 10

Owain Glyndŵr

The fire burns bright

With the death of Llywelyn ap Gruffudd, the last native Prince of Wales in 1282, the Anglo Norman kings of England thought that they had at last conquered Wales, after 216 years of bitter conflict.

True, there were revolts against the tyranny of the conquerors but these tended to be localised and were soon bloodily suppressed. No-one expected the mighty explosion of national feeling that came at the start of the fifteenth century or the upheaval it caused. This too, started as a local revolt but it was not long before it set all of Wales and the borderlands alight in a new war for national freedom.

The course of the war

The beginning

Owain Glyndŵr was a native Welsh lord of royal descent who had lands at Glyndyfrdwy, near Llangollen. He was born around 1355, probably at Sycharth a few miles from Oswestry. Owain was a man of culture and learning, educated at Oxford and at Westminster as a law student. He had been a loyal retainer of Richard II, serving him with distinction as a soldier in France, Scotland and Ireland.

The war started as a boundary dispute with a local Marcher lord, Lord Grey of Ruthin. Since the conquest, the despotic rule and unjust laws of the Norman and English overlords had made it easy to deprive the Welsh of their rights in their own land. Grey, a typical arrogant, land grabbing marcher lord who hated the 'Welch doggis', had seized some of Owain's estate at Glyn Dyfrdwy. Grey had probably seen his opportunity to do this when his close friend Henry IV had usurped the throne and Owain's patron Richard II had been murdered. Owain, for his part, resisted with force and the dispute soon developed into a local revolt. However, such was the widespread economic and social unrest that existed in Wales at the time that his revolt spread like wildfire, attracting men from all social classes, from labourers in the borderlands to students at Oxford and Cambridge. So popular was Owain, that on September 16th 1400, his family and followers met at his estate at Glyn Dyfrdwy, and proclaimed him Prince of Wales. Now the war of independence had truly begun.

The fire spreads

Following the proclamation, the first thing that the rebels did was to attack the town and castle of Ruthin. Soon afterwards, the whole of north-eastern Wales, as far as Oswestry and Welshpool was involved. Then, in the next year, the conflict spread to the Conway valley and beyond into Anglesey and by the end of 1401, all of northern Wales was involved.

Then the rebellion spread southwards. In the spring of 1402 a comet seemed to foretell Owain's success and in the summer the fire of revolt burned in mid Wales where the Welsh on the lands held by the powerful lord marchers, the Mortimers, came over to Owain. By 1403 Glyndŵr was leading his forces into southern Wales so that by the summer of that year most of the south had been brought under his banner. So successful was the rebellion, says Rees in his *Historical Atlas of Wales*, that 'the English settlers everywhere were forced to take shelter within the walled towns or in castles, many of which were closely besieged by the Welsh'. The administration of the Anglo-Norman lordships broke down, and expeditions sent by the king, in 1400, 1401, 1402 and 1403 did little other than relieve the castles.

Glyndŵr the Statesman

Against the great magician, dam'd Glendower.
He durst as well have met the devil alone,
As Owen Glendower for an enemy.

(Shakespeare, Henry IV, Act 1)

In addition to being a brilliant military leader, believed by his enemies to have supernatural powers, Glyndŵr also showed that he was a statesman of vision. He knew that he needed allies outside Wales to help him in his war of independence. To this aim, in 1404, he began to set up the apparatus of a Welsh state and to negotiate alliances with French, Irish and Scottish rulers. The French, in particular, saw Glyndŵr as an important ally in their Hundred Years War against the English. He also sought to renew links with discontented elements in England.

In 1404, with the support of an assembly of his followers at Dolgellau, he signed a treaty with king

Charles VI of France. At this time there were two rival popes in Europe, Boniface IX in Rome, recognised by England, and Benedict XIII in Avignon, acknowledged by France. So, later that year, at an assembly in Pennal, near Machynlleth, Glyndŵr agreed to the French king's suggestion that the Welsh Church be subject to the Avignon Pope. This was done in order to cement the treaty but only on the condition that the church be completely independent of Canterbury and that St David's be elevated to an archbishopric. Furthermore, the Welsh metropolitan area was to include not only Hereford but also the bishoprics of Exeter, Bath, Worcester and Lichfield. However, one of his most visionary proposals was the plan for two universities in Wales, one in the north and one in the south and this some 400 years before the establishment of The University of Wales in the 19th century.

In 1405, now having control over all Wales, he summoned another assembly of his followers at Machynlleth, but this assembly was to be different. This was his historic Parliament, where each commote in Wales had four representatives. Thus Glyndŵr gave Wales democratic government nearly 500 years before the present National Assembly of Wales came into being. Owain's Parliament House still stands today and is open to visitors.

The Tripartite Indenture

Come, here's the map. Shall we divide our right,
According to our threefold order ta'en?

(Shakespeare, Henry IV, Act III)

Early in his campaign, Glyndŵr had already allied himself with the families of Mortimer and Percy as they were hostile to king Henry IV's usurpation of the throne from Richard II. However, this alliance was dealt a severe blow in July 1403, when, in order to join forces with Glyndŵr, the army of Henry Percy or 'Hotspur', moving southwards to cross the Severn near Shrewsbury, was defeated by the king's army, and 'Hotspur' killed in the battle. The alliance was revived in 1405, when Hotspur's father, also Henry Percy, Mortimer and Glyndŵr made an agreement called the 'Tripartite Indenture'. Had this plan succeeded, England as such would have ceased to exist.

The plan involved defeating the king and splitting his realms of England and Wales into three parts. The south of England was to go to Edmund Mortimer, the true heir to the throne of England. The north of England, together with much of the Midlands, to Hotspur's father, the Earl of Northumberland. Glyndŵr was to get a greatly enlarged Wales which would include much of the West Midlands.

Sir John Lloyd in his *'Owen Glendower'*, writes that the compact between the three was sworn and sealed on the 28th of February, 1405 and that 'the boundary of this new Wales is laid down with obvious local knowledge; it runs along the Severn (Gerald's ancient frontier, last chapter) to the north gate of the city of Worcester, thence to the group of ash trees on the high road from Bridgenorth to Kinver known to Welsh fable as "Onennau Meigion" (identified as the hamlet of Six Ashes), thence by the old road running north to the source of the Trent (probably the Staffordshire border), thence to the source of the Mersey and along that river to the sea'. Lloyd comments that not since the 7th century invasion of England by Cadwallon the king of Gwynedd, had a Welsh prince presumed to claim so large an area of England as 'Cambria Irredenta'.

However, there was still much to do before these plans could become reality and the spring of 1405 brought ominous forewarnings. For the first time, Glyndŵr's forces met with heavy defeat at both Grosmont and Usk in Gwent.

The French

The French had promised to send a fleet in 1404, to help Glyndŵr's revolt against English rule in Wales. However, military aid did not come until the summer of 1405, when nearly 3,000 French soldiers arrived in Milford Haven. They were met by 10,000 of Glyndŵr's men. Together, the allies captured Cardigan and Carmarthen before marching eastwards, through southern Wales and Herefordshire to Worcester. Here, they ransacked the suburbs west of the Severn, but faced with a difficult crossing of the river moved to set up camp at Woodberry Hill, some eight miles north-west of Worcester, near Great Witley. In the meantime, King Henry, with his army, having marched from Leicester, had set up camp on another hill across the valley from them, perhaps at Abberley Hill. A possible explanation for Owain's move away from the vicinity of Worcester might be that the king, marching to the north-west of Worcester, had intended to outflank Owain, but that Owain on guessing his intention had moved to intercept him. Here, however, on the 22nd of August, the two armies faced each other across the valley, each waiting for its opponent to attack and start the battle. In the week that followed, over 200 men from each side died in the many skirmishes between the two armies. Many more were wounded, but there was no decisive battle.

By now the allied army was in a desperate situation. Owain had struck too deep into enemy territory and could not renew his supplies. Henry, rather than attack, preferred to let hunger take its toll on the opposing army. Then, on the eighth day, in the belief that he could not win the battle, Henry retreated to the safety of Worcester. As he did so his army was pursued by Owain's men, who managed to capture 18 carts loaded with supplies. However, with the king now safely ensconced in Worcester, and with an army still dangerously low on supplies, Owain's only option was to make an orderly retreat and march back to Wales.

After spending the winter in Wales, the French embarked for home in the spring of 1406. Their expedition had been a complete failure. Neither were Glyndŵr's other allies of any use to him. Scotland wouldn't send help as the Scottish king had been captured by the English and the Earl of Northumberland's revolt in the north of England had failed.

After this, Glyndŵr's star began to wane and little by little the fringes of his kingdom succumbed to the English. By the summer of 1408 Aberystwyth had fallen and only the famous Men of Harlech were left. But, after heroic resistance, even Harlech fell in the spring of 1409. From now until his disappearance around 1413, the struggle became a guerrilla war of raids and ambushes.

Glyndŵr and Hereford

The Military Situation

A post from Wales loaden with heavy news;
Whose worst was, that the noble Mortimer,
leading the men of Herefordshire to fight
Against the irregular and wild Glendower,
Was by the rude hands of that Welshman taken.

(Shakespeare, Henry IV, part 1, Act 1)

In 1402, the great Marcher Lord, Edmund Mortimer whose lands stretched from Ludlow through Wigmore lordship into mid Wales, had led an army to stop Glyndŵr, only to be decisively beaten by him at Pilleth, near Knighton. Mortimer was taken prisoner by Glyndŵr and held for ransom but because Edmund's nephew was a claimant to the throne, Henry IV would not pay, thinking he'd be rid of at least one Mortimer. However, his action backfired because by the end of 1402 Edmund threw in his lot with Owain, married his daughter Catherine and became one of Owain's most loyal supporters until his death fighting for Owain at Harlech in 1409.

Had Owain Glyndŵr won his war of independence, all of the Marches, including Herefordshire could have been in his new Wales. Notwithstanding, everyone in Herefordshire would have known of Glyndŵr anyway. Like all the borderlands the county had for years been in the front line of the war, with the western half being devastated in the fighting and with what appears to have been a determined effort to wrest Archenfield back to Wales by force of arms.

Evidence of the damage caused by Welsh raids which

reached as far as the outskirts of Hereford itself can be seen in the register of Robert Mascall, bishop of Hereford from 1404 to 1416. He reports in 1406 that in his diocese 52 churches had been destroyed, 30 of them in the archdeaconry of Hereford, in the deaneries of Archenfield, Weobley, Leominster and Hereford itself. Naturally, the bishop was concerned only with church property but doubtless there was considerable collateral damage to other property in these villages and townships as well.

A plea by the sheriff of Herefordshire in June, 1404 for the king to send help illustrates some of the panic felt by those in authority. He reports what amounts to an invasion, saying that 'Welsh rebels in great numbers have entered Archenfield, which is part of the county of Hereford, where they have burned houses, killed people, taken prisoners and ravaged the land with great dishonour to the king'. In response the king commanded his son, prince Henry, to organise a counter offensive from his base in Worcester.

Geoffrey Hodges, in his *'Owain Glyndŵr'*, believes that although the raids only directly affected the west of the county, the effect on morale extended far beyond. It caused such a feeling of insecurity that people in Herefordshire (and Shropshire as well) felt compelled to make their own treaties with the Welsh, paying them taxes which really amounted to 'protection money' in order to escape their attentions.

Herefordshire was also on the route of the Franco-Welsh march to Worcester in 1405. The outward march was through Glamorgan and Gwent, passing Newport, Usk and Monmouth, before entering Archenfield, which may still have been under Welsh control at this date, before crossing the Wye by Ross, and moving up the eastern part of the county towards Worcester. After the debacle there, the allied army retreated across northern Herefordshire through Leominster and Weobley to Hay and thence south-west. Hodges, believes that although the hungry retreating army may have stopped at Leominster on its route, a truce was struck, with the locals providing supplies as long there was no looting. The army would not have loitered anyway, as king Henry had called for a general muster of forces at Hereford, thus endangering the retreat to Wales.

The last act

Even with his citadels lost, Owain was far from beaten and continued to wage a vigorous guerrilla war. Evidence of this is shown in 1407 when Parliament called on the Lords Marcher to defend their own lands and castles. Again, in May, 1409 letters were sent to the absentee Marcher Lords of Ewyas Lacy, Oswestry, Powys, Gower, Ruthin, Maelienydd, Glamorgan, Pembroke and Abergavenny, in which they were ordered to reside in their Welsh domains and castles and devote themselves to suppressing the Welsh revolt. Glyndŵr was reported to still have a large following, with French and Scottish helpers, and to be causing devastation far and wide.

Owain's last major attempt to change the course of the war was a great attack on Shrewsbury in 1410. This was a disaster. Not only were his forces driven back, but three of his best captains, Rhys ap Gruffydd of Cardigan, Philip Scudamore of Troy near Monmouth and Rhys ap Tudur, Owain's cousin were captured and executed. However, even as late as June 1412, he managed to capture a Dafydd Gam of the Lordship of Brecknock and hold him for ransom. This was one of his last acts. By 1413, although sporadic resistance continued, the great leader had vanished.

By 1415, prince Henry had become king Henry V and, being more interested in conquests in France than in hunting down the Welsh rebels, offered free pardons to Glyndŵr and his remaining supporters provided they swore obedience to him. This offer was not taken up by Owain, even when it was repeated in 1416. In 1417, Owain's son Maredudd accepted a pardon on the 30th of April, but there was no sign of the old warrior, and he was presumed dead.

His final resting place?

Since 1400, Owain had been surrounded in mystery, his enemies believing him to be a magician who could command the weather to fight against them. His sudden disappearance was well in keeping with this mystical tradition. Prophets said that he was not dead and they even foretold of his victorious return. Like Arthur, Owain became a legend, with his people awaiting his return. Thus, the actual date and place of his death can only be gleaned from local hearsay and tradition. Probably the strongest of these traditions is that he spent his last days in Hereford, but exactly where is still the subject of debate.

One writer, Kingsford, in his *Life Of King Henry*, says that Owain died on the hill at Lawton's Hope, near Dinemore Manor, not far from Leominster. Another, Price, in his *History of Leominster*, that Owain met his end in Haywood Forest, near Callow a few miles to the south of Hereford. Both considered him to be a brigand chief, a rebel and an outlaw, and a miserable death as a wandering outcast could be more a reflection of their attitudes than actual fact. A happier and far more convincing story is that he spent his last years living with one of his daughters who had married into a Herefordshire family, and died on the 20th of September 1416.

Although most writers believe that Owain spent his remaining years with his daughter Alice and her husband, Sir John Scudamore, at Monnington Straddle in the Golden Valley near Vowchurch, some confusion has arisen over the name Monnington, since another daughter, Margaret, had married a Roger Monnington, who was a tenant at Monnington on Wye. Although, as several writers have pointed out, whilst Monnington Straddle was in Ewyas Harold in a Welsh speaking area, sympathetic to Owain, Monnington on Wye was not. It was on the other side of the Wye in hostile territory and Owain would have had to cross the river in order to evade any attempt to arrest him. Also, at Monnington Straddle, Sir John Scudamore who had some influence would have been able to protect Owain from the authorities.

Sir John also had another manor at Kentchurch, in the quiet Monnow Valley, near Pontrilas. Kentchurch is in Archenfield, another Welsh speaking area. At this manor there is a tower where according to local tradition, Owain is said to have stayed. Geoffrey Hodges believes it would have been more likely for Owain to stay at this manor, rather than Monnington Straddle, as it was more secluded. However, it was very close to Grosemont Castle and its garrison. Although Lloyd on the other hand, plumps for Monnington Straddle in the Golden Valley it's quite reasonable to assume that Owain spent time in both manors. It is interesting to note that near the present Monnington Court there is a mound of earth which is either the remains of an older moated manor or those of a castle and which, again according to folklore could contain Owain's grave.

Another of his daughters, Janet, lived in Croft Castle near Mortimers Cross in the north of the county and Owen Croft, a descendent, argues in favour of Croft Castle, saying that it was secluded and easy to escape from. However, it is likely that the locals would have been hostile to Glyndŵr because, after all, many of their kin would have died in battles such as Pilleth in 1402. Consequently, Owain would have been far safer in the Scudamore manors, in Welsh speaking Hereford than here.

Geoffrey Hodges puts forward a possible explanation to link the various claims. He says that Owain, while staying with Alice and knowing he was ill and close to death, might have wished to see Janet before he died. On his way back from Croft, he became ill and died at Lawton's Hope. Alternatively, he may have wished to see Margaret as well as Janet and perhaps died in Haywood forest after crossing the Wye on his return, his body being brought back to Monnington or Kentchurch for burial. What a wonderful plot for a play or a novel!

Today, there is a society whose members wish to find Owain's grave and bring his remains back to Wales. However, this would be wrong. If Owain was buried at Monnington or Kentchuch, it was in Wales for him, Hereford in Wales.

Booklist:

Owain Glyndŵr & The War of Independence in the Welsh Borders, by Geoffrey Hodges, pub. by Logaston Press 1995, chapters 5,9,11.

An Historical Atlas of Wales, from Early to Modern Times, by William Rees, pub. Faber & Faber 3 Queen Square, London, 1972.

Owen Glendower, Sir John E. Lloyd, Oxford University Press, 1931, reprinted by Llanerch Publishers, Felinfach, 1992.

General reading:

Famous Welshmen, Cardiff University of Wales Press, 1974.

Wales in History, Book II – 1066-1485, The Defenders, by David Fraser, pub. by University of Wales Press, Cardiff, 1967.

History of England and Wales, From the Earliest Times to 1485, by Howell T. Evans, M.A., pub. by The educational publishing Co.Ltd., Trade Street, Cardiff, 1908.

Princes and People of Wales, by John Miles, pub by The Starling Press Ltd., Risca, Newport, Gwent, 1977.

The King's England, Herefordshire, edited by Arthur Mee, pub. Hodder and Stoughton, London, 1948.

The History of Ewias Harold, by The Rev. A.T. Bannister, Jakeman & Carver, Hereford, 1902.

Chapter 11

The Son of Prophecy?

Duped

The bards of the Britons had, since the earliest Saxon invasions, prophesied that a hero would come one day to save them from the barbarian. They called this hero 'The Son Of the Prophecy', in Welsh 'Y Mab Darogan'. Some said this hero was Arthur and that one day he would return to rule all of Britain. When Owain appeared, the bards and seers thought that here at last was the 'Mab Darogan', but it was not to be and when Owain disappeared these seers said that one day he would return to liberate his people.

Thus, when in 1485 Henry Tudor, the Duke of Richmond, a nobleman of Welsh descent, landed in western Wales, the Welsh saw him as the fulfilment of the prophecy and flocked to his banner in their thousands. Without this Welsh support, Henry could not have won the battle of Bosworth and become Henry VII. Yet, with all his other problems, Henry would have little time for Wales, and his son Henry VIII would turn the prophecy on its head.

Henry VII, Wales and the March

Family origins

Henry Tudor's victory over Richard III at Bosworth in 1485 was claimed a Welsh triumph by Tudor propagandists. Indeed, Henry was of Welsh descent. His grandfather, Owain Tudor, came from a long established family of the Welsh gentry from Penmynydd, Anglesey. The family had supported Glyndŵr. In about 1425, after seeing service in France, Owain, said to be 'a beautiful person' with 'many gifts of nature', became a courtier as the Keeper of the Wardrobe of Queen Catherine, the French widow of Henry V. After what was rumoured to be a torrid love affair, Catherine, against all advice, secretly married Owain, a commoner in 1429. They had three sons, Edmund, Jasper and Owain, who became a monk.

In 1455, Edmund had married the twelve year old Margaret Beaufort a descendent of John o Gaunt. With the extinction of the male line of the Beauforts, the Beaufort claim to the throne devolved on Margaret and Edmund. However, with Margaret pregnant, Edmund died suddenly in November, 1456. In the following January at Pembroke castle, under the protection of Jasper, Margaret gave birth to a son, whom she called Henry.

Defeat and Victory

Henry was born soon after the start of the terrible dynastic civil war, known as the Wars of the Roses. The two factions were the Lancastrians to which the infant Henry belonged and which wore a red rose as its emblem and the Yorkists who wore a white rose.

A series of battles proved indecisive. Then, early in

1461 Jasper Tudor led a Lancastrian army into battle at Mortimer's Cross near Leominster. The Yorkists were led by Edward of York, the future Edward IV. It was a total rout for the Lancastrians and Jasper was lucky to escape with his life. His father Owain was not so lucky, neither was Sir John Scudamore of the Golden Valley and his sons*, sons of Alice and grandsons of Glyndŵr. Edward was merciless. They and other Lancastrian captains who were captured, were, on February 3rd, taken to the market place at Hereford where they were beheaded. One account, in the 15th century Gregory's Chronicle, states that Owain's head was displayed upon the highest step in the market place, where a mad woman combed his hair and washed the blood from his face before lighting over a hundred candles and setting them around the head, the head that at one time was wont to lie in Queen Catherine's lap. His body was buried in a now lost Church of the Grey Friars, Hereford.

(*Note: *Gregory mentions a knight and his two sons; Arthur Mee says it was Sir John and his three sons*)

Jasper continued to fight on after this but defeat followed defeat until, in 1471, he was forced to flee into exile to Brittany taking Margaret and the young Henry with him. It was during his exile that Henry was chosen by the Lancastrians as their claimant to the throne. The exile was to last for fourteen years until Edward IV had died and his successor Richard III's misrule made the time ripe for a return.

Jasper, Henry and a small force landed at Milford Haven on 25th August 1485, with the red dragon of Wales as their standard, to receive a tumultuous reception from the Welsh who saw in Henry the fulfilment of the old prophecy. Now an army of Welshmen marched with him up through western and mid-Wales, on past Shrewsbury to Bosworth Field where king Richard died and the new king Henry Tudor became the founder of a dynasty.

Henry and Wales

We will unite the white rose and the red:
Smile Heaven upon this fair conjunction,
That long hath frown'd upon their enmity!
What traitor hears me, and says not Amen?

(Shakespeare, Richard III, Act V)

During his reign Henry's main concern was to consolidate his hold on the throne and restore order to his kingdom as a whole. To this end one of his first steps was to unite the two warring factions in the War of the Roses by marrying Elizabeth of York. He also set up the powerful Court of Star Chamber which he used to suppress the power of the great lords, whom he saw as a constant threat to his rule. This indirectly helped Wales in that it helped to curb the Marcher lords whose private feuds had caused so much misery and ruin.

In Wales itself, Henry rewarded those who had followed him to Bosworth with land, titles and office. He also encouraged the growth of the Welsh gentry class from which much of his support had come, by granting them exemptions from the penal restrictions* the Welsh had suffered as a result of Glyndŵr's War of Independence. He also re-established the Council for Wales and the Marches in an attempt to bring law and order to the March of Wales, the most lawless part of his realm.

(***Note on the Penal Statutes:** Henry did nothing to repeal the statutes most hated by the Welsh and passed in Henry IV's reign to punish the Welsh for Glyndŵr's war. It was illegal for a Welshman to buy land in England or the English boroughs in Wales, to hold office in England, or for an Englishman to marry a Welsh woman without losing his privileged status. The more ambitious Welshmen paid to become naturalised Englishmen, governed by the laws of England and not by the thraldom and cruelty used by the Marcher lords.)

The March of Wales

After Edward I's conquest, in 1282 Wales had been divided into two parts, the Principality and the March. The Principality belonged to the Crown and was organised into shires which were administered along similar lines to English shires although some aspects of Hywel Dda's ancient laws survived, such as those of inheritance. In contrast, the other part of Wales, the March had no uniform administration whatsoever. It consisted of a large number of lordships each with its own laws. Here, the only authority recognised was that of the immediate lord himself, whose privileges were extensive and largely undefined. The lord had his own seal, courts and chancery, and was the only source of justice, making his own laws and levying his own taxes. Only in exceptional circumstances could the king's officers interfere. In short, the lord was practically a king in his own lordship.

These lordships were often the haunts of brigands whom the lord hired to fight in his private feuds or to raid his neighbours. Also, as a direct result of the chaos caused by the Wars of the Roses, banditry was rife. Life and property were in constant danger. Criminals could not be arrested in one lordship for crimes they had committed in another. Murders, burnings, rustling and theft were frequent in both Wales and the neighbouring English shires. The smaller Welsh tenants suffered most, by being constantly oppressed by corrupt and heartless officials of the local lord and daily liable to being set upon by criminals. The Marches were truly the most lawless part of Henry's realm with the grievances here being far worse than those of the Welsh in the Principality where the chief complaint was the brutal conduct of royal officials.

The Council of the Principality and the March of Wales

No one knew the state of the Marches better than the Yorkist Edward IV who had inherited the Mortimer estates. It was he who made the first attempt to deal with the situation. He set up a commission at Hereford, out of which the Court of the Council of the Principality and the March of Wales was established at Ludlow in 1478. The Council was to last in different forms until 1689.

Henry revived the Council which had its own court, president and lawyers. Its purpose was to establish firm government in the Principality and the March of Wales, or, as the Elizabethan writer William Gerrard put it, to act as a check on rebellion in Wales, to curb lawlessness and to relieve the oppression of the poor. As it was also intended to defend the border counties of Herefordshire, Shropshire, Worcestershire and Gloucestershire from cross border raiding, the Council's authority extended over these counties as well.

In 1501, Henry's eldest son Arthur, the fifteen year old Prince of Wales, became president of the Council and brought his new wife, Catherine of Aragon, to Ludlow. Unfortunately, Arthur died five months later and although the Council remained in existence, it would be another thirty years before it had a president who would make it an effective force in the Marches.

Henry VIII and The Act Of Union

Henry VIII's Revolution

When Henry VII died in 1509, he was succeeded by his 18 years old son, Henry, who became Henry VIII. In order to preserve the alliance with Spain, the young king had married Arthur's widow, Catherine of Aragon, and for twenty years ruled in much the same fashion as his father before him. Then in 1529, with no male heir by Catherine, Henry who had never been altogether satisfied about the validity of their marriage, requested a divorce in order that he could marry the beautiful Anne Boleyn. What followed was one of the greatest revolutions in English history.

Henry ordered his minister, Cardinal Wolsey to arrange the annulment. But ultimately, only the Pope could annul the marriage and the Pope was in the power of Catherine's nephew, Charles, the king of Spain and Holy Roman Emperor. All the Pope could do was to avoid granting a divorce for as long as possible. Henry's anxieties about his succession and the validity of his marriage coupled with his desire to marry Anne Bolyn, with whom he had become besotted, made him extremely impatient with this delay. As Wolsey could do nothing, Henry angrily dismissed him.

Because the Pope was unable to annul his marriage to Catherine, Henry now more convinced than ever in the rightness of his request, determined to explore other means in order to get his desired divorce. However, it became increasingly obvious that the only means open to him involved the separation of the Church in England from Rome. Regretfully, he summoned Parliament, which in 1534 passed the Act of Supremacy which gave Henry the title of Supreme Head on Earth of the Church of England. He wasted no time in having his marriage to Catherine declared 'contrary to the law of God'.

In the events that followed 1529, Henry rid himself of all of those ministers and advisers who had stood in his way. His new advisers would be only those who would aid him in his plans and follow his orders. The ambitious opportunist, Thomas Cromwell, who was said by his enemies to have a satanic influence on the king, came to the fore as Henry's chief adviser, second in power only to the king. He showed himself to be an able man, devoted to the king's interests. It was he who was Henry's main instrument in the dissolution of the many monasteries in order to acquire their considerable wealth.

The Hanging Bishop

Until the coming of Cromwell, little had changed in the Marches. They were still the most lawless part of Henry's realms. Then, in 1532 Cromwell appointed Rowland Lee, Bishop of Lichfield as president of the Council of the Principality and March of Wales. He was a very strange sort of clergyman. He delighted in hanging felons publicly on market days, believing that such gruesome spectacles deterred others. He especially enjoyed executing gentlemen, as he believed that hanging one gentleman was better than hanging a hundred petty wretches. He would tour the borders to carry out his work. For instance, in 1534 he was reported as being busy at Hereford in July, Shrewsbury in August, Ludlow in November and Presteigne in December. In six years he is reported to have hanged over 5,000 miscreants. Even if this figure was exaggerated, it demonstrates his terrible reputation in the Marches. Lee was helped by several Acts of Parliament. Severe punishment for perjury or the bribery or intimidation of juries was introduced. There was tighter control of the ferries across the Severn to prevent the escape of felons and anyone involved in ambushing officers in pursuit of felons became felons themselves.

The Act of Union 1536

The distress of the people is incredible, especially the Welsh, from whom by Act of Parliament the king has just taken away their native laws, customs and privileges.

> From a letter to the king of Spain
> from Eustace Chapuys, 1536.

Before Henry's divorce from Catherine, Spain had been an ally. But in 1534 there was increasing concern that France and Spain, wanting to see the Pope's authority restored, might unite and invade England and that Scotland could join them. There were also disturbing rumours that this invasion could come through Wales, where the Welsh people and some of the Marcher lords who sought a return to the Roman Catholic faith would gladly support it.

Cromwell, perhaps recalling Glyndŵr's Franco-Welsh invasion, realised that the suppression of lawlessness in the Welsh March would not, in itself, be enough. In order to make Henry secure on the throne, the king had to have total control over every part of his kingdom. The differences of language, law and religion in Wales had to go. Wales had to be 'incorporated, united and annexed with the realm of England', and in order to do this there was a need to 'utterly extirp all and singular the sinister usages and customs differing from the same (those of England)', and bring 'his said dominion of Wales to an amiable concord and unity'.

As a result, in 1536, 'the Act of Union' was passed. Wales was divided into 13 shires, based on the English model. Each shire was to have a sheriff and justices of the peace and the Welsh gentry would be able to send MPs to Westminster. Most of the Marcher lordships would be merged to form seven new counties to add to the six of the Principality. However, some lordships would be lost to England, with the new arrangements isolating Welsh speaking communities such as Oswestry and Ewyas on the wrong side of the new boundaries. Wales would no longer legally exist and English would now be the only official language of law and administration in Wales, regardless of the fact that the vast majority of the people spoke only Welsh. This, however, did not matter to Cromwell. The Welsh language with its rich and ancient literature was henceforth to be treated as a patois to be 'extirped'.

A greater Herefordshire

Herefordshire gained a considerable amount of territory in the west as a result of the Act of Union.

' . . . the lordships, towns, parishes, commotes, hundreds and cantreds of **Ewyas Lacy, Ewyas Harold, Clifford, Wynforton, Eardisley, Huntington, Whitney, Wigmore, Logharneys and Stapleton** *in the said marches of Wales . . . thereof shall stand and be forever after*

> *the said feast of All Saints gildable, and shall be united, annexed and joined with the county of Hereford . . . '*

The above lordships were to be formed into hundreds, each of which would be treated no differently to any other hundred in Herefordshire. 'All previous liberties, franchises and privileges' were lost. The lordships of Wigmore and Logharneys (or Lougharness an alternative name for Stapleton) were to form the new hundred of Wigmore*. Ewyas Lacy became the hundred of Ewias Lacy. Ewyas Harold became part of the hundred of Webtree. Clifford, Wynforton, Eardisley, Whitney and Huntington became the new hundred of Huntington.

(***Note:** 'Wigmore' = Welsh 'Y Wig Mawr', *The Great Forest*)

Gloucester gained the lordships, towns and parishes of Wollaston, Tidenham and Beachley, which had been part of the lordship of Strigoil (an old name for Chepstow). These became part of the hundred of Westbury.

A betrayal of trust

The Welsh had greeted Henry VII's victory at Bosworth with jubilation. Here at last was a Welsh king who would surely bring justice and freedom to his people and honour his native land, its language and its culture. Yet, although Henry made a few symbolic gestures such as naming his eldest son Arthur and flying the red dragon banner at court, the only Welsh people to really benefit from his accession were the gentry. These, who had in the past been the patrons of the Welsh language and culture, had now become dependent on the king in London for their future prosperity, and become increasingly alienated from the mass of the Welsh people in the process.

Thus when Henry VII's son decided to annex and assimilate Wales, and its people were to be ruled, judged and preached to* in a language that they didn't understand, there was no one to lead a protest. Howell T. Evans in his *History of England and Wales* writes that 'If they (the Welsh) had wished to rebel, they would have found no leaders among the gentry to whom in former days they had been accustomed to look for leadership, for the latter had become rich with the spoils of the monasteries.' There was to be no new Glyndŵr to lead them to a new Wales. Those who led Welsh society in the 16th century, the Welsh gentry, had sold out and were in full collaboration with the government in London.

(***Note:** The new Bibles of the Reformed Church of England were in English only. Henry VIII had refused to allow a Welsh translation)*

Booklist:
Lancaster and York; The Wars of the Roses, by Alison Weir, pub. Jonathan Cape, London, 1995.
History of England and Wales; From1485 to 1910, vol.2, by Howell T. Evans, pub. The Educational Publishing Co Ltd., Cardiff/London.
An Historical Atlas of Wales, by William Rees, pub. Faber& Faber, London, 1972.
The Union of England and Wales. Article by William Rees, and copy of the Act in Transactions of the Honourable Society of Cymmrodorion, Session 1937-1938.
History of Wales, Volume III, Recovery, Reorientation and Reformation – Wales c1415-1642, by Glanmor Williams, pub. Claredon Press, Oxford. University of Wales Press, 1987.
Modern Wales, a concise history, by Gareth Elwyn Jones,

pub. by Cambridge University Press, 2nd edition, 1994.

The King's England; Herefordshire, ed. Arthur Mee, pub. Hodder and Stoughton, London. 1948.

The Battles of Wales, by Dilys Gater, Gwasg Carreg Gwalch, Llanrwst, 1991.

Lives and Letters of the Great Tudor Dynasties; Rivals in power, ed. by David Starkey, pub. Macmillan, London, 1990.

Outlines of British History, Part 1 The Beginnings to 1603, by F.W. Tickner, University of London Press Ltd., London 1925, for information on Henry VII's divorce.

Chapter 12

The Heritage

A rich Celtic heritage.

For a long time after the Act Of Union, much of Herefordshire remained within the orbit of Welsh cultural influences. The Welsh language was widely spoken down to the 19th century and the county witnessed at first hand both the advent of the Welsh Bible in the 16th century and the Welsh Nonconformist Movement in the 17th and 18th centuries. Family ties with the neighbouring Welsh border counties were still strong and Welsh drovers crossed the county with their herds of cattle. Welsh people came to work and live in both the city and the countryside, something that they still do today.

The Welsh Bible in Hereford in the 16th century

There are four Dioceses of Bishops in Wales, if Hereford be accounted in England, according to the new descriptions.

Polydore Vergil, 1513

The Reformation

When Protestant Elizabeth succeeded her Catholic sister, Mary, in 1558, she believed that it was essential that the Reformation started by her father, Henry VIII, get back on course in order to secure her own place on the throne. The dangers of Counter Reformation and invasion from Spain were ever present. If Philip of Spain were to invade, Elizabeth herself would soon be replaced by Mary Stuart, Queen of the Scots. Thus, in order to ensure the loyalty of all her subjects, the Reformation of the Church of England, with Elizabeth as Head of that Church, had to succeed.

Yet in Wales, there was a danger of Counter Reformation. The people were at best indifferent to the reformers. The Welsh had been familiar with the old Latin service, even if they hadn't fully understood it. In contrast, the English Bible and service, as decreed by Henry VIII, were both alien and incomprehensible to them. Church leaders had already realised that to win Wales for the Reformation, it would be necessary to instruct the people in the language that they understood and now persuaded Elizabeth to allow them to do so.

As a result, in 1563, Parliament passed an Act to provide for the translation of both the Bible and the Book of Common Prayer into Welsh. The bishops of Bangor, Llandaf, St Asaph's, St David's and Hereford were to see that this was done and that at least one copy of each was placed in every church in their dioceses by St David's Day, March 1st, 1567. Failure to so provide would mean a penalty of £40 for each bishop. Also, from that date, the service was to be in Welsh, 'where that tongue was commonly spoken or used'.

In the troubled times of the second half of the 16th century Hereford would not have been included in the

1563 Act had there not been a substantial number of Welsh speakers there. Further, David Williams in his *History of Modern Wales* says that there is ample evidence that the ecclesiastical authorities considered it desirable that the lower clergy, drawn from the people, should speak Welsh, even in the border parishes within the diocese of Hereford.

At first, only translations of the New Testament and the Book of Common Prayer were available in Welsh. The translation of the Bible in full didn't appear until the famous Bishop Morgan translation of 1588.

The authorities had never actually intended the translations to be anything more than a temporary measure. Elizabeth and her advisors had been persuaded that the provision of Welsh versions would more easily facilitate the learning of English. By placing a copy of the Bible and Book of Common Prayer in English alongside the Welsh versions in each church they believed that those reading them together would 'by conferring in both languages together, the sooner attain a knowledge of the English tongue'.

However, in the event, the effect of Bishop Morgan's Bible was quite different. It probably saved Welsh from extinction by providing a standardised form of the language which prevented it from degenerating into a series of widely differing local dialects.

Welsh Nonconformity in the 17th and 18th centuries

Just as Archenfield and Ewyas played a leading role in the religious revolution of the 5th and 6th centuries, so were they in the forefront of the establishment of the Welsh Nonconformist Movement in the 17th and 18th centuries. Founders of both the Baptist and Calvinistic Methodist Churches in Wales considered western Hereford to be well within their orbit.

The Baptists

A Carmarthenshire man, Joshua Thomas, who was the Baptist minister of Etnam Street Church, Leominster from 1753 to 1797, wrote a history of the early Welsh Baptist Movement. In it, Thomas, keen to boost the Baptist cause, claimed that a Baptist Church in the Olchon Valley, Ewyas, established in 1633, was the Mother Church of all Welsh Nonconformity. Certainly it was one of the earliest Welsh Baptist congregations and in 1794 the Baptist Cymanfa Ddeheol (Religious Singing Festival for South Wales) was held there. Even as late as 1875 one Morgan Lewis occasionally preached there in Welsh.

In 1646 there were many Baptists in Cromwell's army and they preached against infant baptism throughout the borderlands. Thus, as Geraint Jenkins says, in his *Protestant Dissenters in Wales*, many people and certainly those in the Welsh speaking parts of Herefordshire turned their backs on the ungodly world to form communities of saints and practise believers' baptism. These conversions in their turn contributed to a collapse of support for the royalist cause in the borders.

The Methodist Revival

In the 18th century, western Hereford was to witness the Great Welsh Methodist Revival at first hand in the person of Howell Harris, one of the main leaders of the Revival. Harris, born at Trefecca, near Talgarth, in Breconshire, had intended to enter the Established Church. However, in 1735, a sermon by the Rev. Pryce Davies, vicar of Talgarth, urging people to attend Whit Sunday

Communion, changed his life and set him on fire with an enthusiasm to preach to people in the area, warning them of their sins. This offended the vicar, who now refused to recommend Howell for ordination. However, although Howell tried to repress his zeal by becoming a schoolteacher, it was not long before he was out preaching again, travelling from his base in Trefecca over a wide area of south-eastern Wales and the nearby parts of Herefordshire. The people of a district would hear of him and then invite him to preach to them. Later, they would establish a community of converts.

In 1737, he met Daniel Rowland, another evangelist, and together they joined forces to create a powerful religious movement.

Harris made many visits into the then Welsh speaking parts of Hereford, although in the borders, he would often address his congregations in both languages. In 1737, he was invited to preach at Longtown, where he had a rapturous reception. Then in January 1738, in Olchon, he addressed a huge congregation of more than 800 people for over six hours in both Welsh and English. However, such a rigorous pace sometimes proved too much for him. Thus, one Saturday in June, 1738, he had travelled over such a wide area of Herefordshire, preaching in various places for over seven hours, in both Welsh and English, that the experience exhausted him to the extent that he failed to arrive at his Sunday morning service the next day.

Until 1811, when the Calvinistic Methodist Church was formally established, the Revival, although still nominally within the Established Church, was basically interdenominational. The outcome was that Harris had many friendly contacts with other Nonconformist churches in the borders. One such contact was James

Roberts, a Baptist minister in Ross who became a close and lasting friend and convert to the Movement.

The Drovers

The bleak, windswept hills that form much of Wales are too cold and wet for crop growing. Consequently, livestock rearing has always been the mainstay of Welsh farming. Since the Middle Ages, there had been a growing market for this livestock in England, especially so when a steady supply of meat became an important factor in the growth of London in later centuries. The Welsh drovers with their herds of cattle or sheep became an increasingly common sight on the roads and trackways of the Midlands and southern England as they took them to the lucrative markets of Barnet or Smithfield. The trade became so important that in north Wales Archbishop John Williams likened it to the 'Spanish Fleet', bringing back gold.

There were three main routes. The northern drovers went through Cheshire, those from the central highlands passed Shrewsbury, along the Severn valley, whilst those from the more southerly hills came through Herefordshire. Whilst in the county, they might sometimes stop to sell their animals in Leominster and other towns, including the city of Hereford itself. Mostly though, they would only stop to fatten their lean mountain stock on the county's lush lowland grass before again moving eastwards. It was a growing trade, with tens of thousands of animals being moved. By the mid 18th century more than 30,000 cattle and sheep were leaving Wales to cross Herefordshire each year.

Like the later cowboys in America, the Welsh drovers were a rugged breed, with a dirty, dangerous job which involved many hardships. Yet, although they spent weeks on the road, they were not rough, uneducated drifters. On the contrary, in order to get an annual licence to trade in cattle the drovers had to be numerate, literate, and mature married householders. They had to have these qualifications and also be trustworthy, because in their trading activities they handled large sums of money, took rents to absentee landlords and acted as unofficial bankers for the ordinary people. A few absconded with other people's money, but most were honest and well trusted. One such drover, a man called Llwyd, was the founder of Lloyd's Bank.

With the coming of the 19th century, came the railways and by the second half of the century the drovers were virtually redundant.

The Welsh Language in the 18th and 19th centuries

The Extent of Welsh in 1485
In 1892, in his book, *Wales and Her Language,* John E. Southall, himself a Herefordshire man born, as he says, 'some 18 miles east of Offa's Dyke, but within sight of the Welsh hills in Radnor and Brecon', hypothesizes, from his own extensive research into the matter, the extent of the language in 1485, the year of Henry VII's accession. He says that in nearly all of Herefordshire, west of the Wye and north and east of the Wye from Yazor to Leintwardine (i.e. the Marcher Lordships), and in that part of the Forest of Dean next to the Wye, namely the 'Cantref Coch' (Red Hundred), over 60% of the population would have been Welsh speaking. Ewyas and Archenfield, around Ross, were almost solidly Welsh

speaking. In addition to this, he believed that some Welsh, but less than 60%, was spoken over a much wider area of Herefordshire, east of the Wye and Gloucestershire, 'nearly up to Gloucester Bridge'.

From this the history of the Welsh language in both Herefordshire and Gloucester would seem to be one of gradual recession westwards. However, this recession would have been slower in some areas than others. Thus by the close of the19th century, whilst Archenfield and the eastern fringe of Gwent had become English speaking, Welsh was still spoken in the Olchon Valley and in the north of Gwent, including Abergavenny.

Welsh in Ewyas

In his own day (i.e. 1892), Southall surveyed the extent of the Welsh language throughout Wales and the Marches. He says that 'to acquire the necessary information for this purpose, it was necessary to enter on some correspondence with persons possessing special opportunities of information (local knowledge), and as well, to visit certain districts myself'. As regards Herefordshire in his own day, he remarks that 'the last flickering flames of a knowledge of Welsh still lingered in south-western Herefordshire'.

According to his informants, Welsh was still understood by about a third of the population in Olchon and Longtown, and at Newton in the Dulas valley, 4 miles up from Ewyas Harold, the children at the Board School were taught Welsh songs. However, when he actually visited Longtown, he found that although the language was no longer spoken there, it had still been in use some 30 years before that (i.e. around 1860), and one farmer near Longtown told him that 60 years previously nearly everyone spoke Welsh, but that 'they did not teach the children Welsh'. The farmer added that he would very much have liked to learn Welsh. Further up, at Olchon House, he found a farm servant who could understand and speak a little Welsh and who said that there were others like him locally. Therefore it is highly probable that some Welsh speakers in the Olchon Valley survived into the 20th century.

Welsh in Archenfield

Although native Welsh does not appear to have been spoken in Archenfield at the time of Southall's survey, there is evidence of its survival there at least until the second half of the 18th century. In 1707, Edward Lhuyd comments that the Gwentian dialect of Welsh was used there and John Matthews in his *History of Wormelow* writes that Welsh was still spoken in the Kentchurch area circa 1750. More vaguely, Matthews says that 'In 1867 Welsh was still spoken within 20 miles of Hereford'. Place name evidence also indicates the recent survival of Welsh. In an article for the 'O'Donnell Lectures, Angles and Britons', 1963, B.G. Charles writes that the distribution of minor place-names, such as the names of farms, hills, dales, fields etc., in Archenfield suggests the survival of Welsh in the heart of the area, 'well into modern times'.

Elsewhere in Hereford, we return to Southall, who reports that one elderly informant surprised him, by saying that in 1835 he had conversed in Welsh with the mistress of a farm at Yazor, north of the Wye some 8 miles north-west of Hereford. She had assured him that in her childhood, the children generally spoke Welsh. As for Hereford itself, Southall quotes evidence in the SPCK Diocesan History which says that in 1642 many in the city spoke Welsh as their native language.

Other sources report the official use of Welsh in the city, such as at a trial of nine men for murder at Hereford in 1770 when a number of the accused could not speak English and a Welsh interpreter had to be brought in. Also, as late as 1855 the clerk to the Hereford Magistrates was chosen because he could speak Welsh.

Welsh in the Forest of Dean

Here I can relate something that I learnt at first hand, purely by chance. During the 1990s, I was teaching in a Cardiff school, where one of my colleagues happened to be a lady whose family had lived in the Cinderford area of the Forest. On hearing of my interest in the borders, she told me that her grandmother had often told her that her own grandmother and her family had been Welsh speaking. However, my informant's grandmother had insisted that her family were not Welsh. Allowing say 25 years for each generation, and estimating that my informant had been born in the 1950s, her grandmother would have been born in the 1900s, and her grandmother in the 1850s. The grandmother's insistence on not being Welsh is interesting in that it indicates the social pressure on Welsh speakers to be English and could explain the speed of the language's decline there in the 19th century. Similar pressures to conform to an English norm were at work in Wales itself until recently. In the Forest of Dean, though, there is a possibility that this family could originally have come from Wales to seek work in the coalmines. Such speculation opens the door to the further possibility that there could have been a steady flow of Welsh speaking mining families into the Forest throughout the 19th century.

Welsh Hereford into the 20th century

Writing in 1912, in his *History of Wormelow*, John Matthews says that Welsh Herefordshire is comprised of the south western hundreds of Wormelow (*Archenfield), Webtree and Ewyas Lacy. He comments that prior to 1881 there had been a teeming population of Silures there, but that this had been much reduced over the previous thirty years by migration, 'facilitated by modern means of locomotion', namely the railway. People had gone to 'Cardiff, Bristol, Birmingham, London, the Colonies and even the States'.

Yet, in spite of this decline, he still concluded that the indigenous population of south-western Hereford remained Welsh in his day and that the Wye was still the boundary between Briton and Saxon.

***Note:** Matthews explains that during the 14th century, Archenfield had come to be known as the Hundred of Wormelow. Previously Wormelow had been a part of Archenfield.*

Conclusion

The Heritage, Today and Tomorrow

The concept of 'nation' provided modern historians with a convenient framework around which to organise their materials, but a price had to be paid. What became later national boundaries were extended backwards into a past where they had little or no relevance, with the consequence that the earlier tribal or pre-national societies were lost to sight. The border between 'Wales' and 'England' is a case in point. It is now assumed that Herefordshire and Shropshire are part of 'England' and that their inhabitants are 'English', with all the appropriate 'mental furniture' to go with that term. In fact these border counties have been the scene of intermingling between 'Welsh' and 'English' cultures over a long period of time.

Hugh Kearney, The British Isles, 1989

Now, although the drovers have gone, there are still many Welsh people living and working in Herefordshire and thousands of Welsh visitors come each year. Welsh accents are common and the Welsh language might even still be heard in the streets. There is even a thriving Welsh Club in Hereford itself, and I know of at least one learners' group, called Clwb Clebran (Welsh Chat Club), in Ross. However, such manifestations are usually associated with expatriate Welsh and not with locally born people. Yet, what Matthews said in 1912 about the indigenous population west of the Wye being basically Welsh, still holds true today, and probably holds true for all of western Herefordshire. Local family names such as Watkins, Edwards, Jones, Thomas, Lewis etc. all reflect old family ties further west. Why then is there a general lack of awareness of the county's rich Celtic heritage in the present day? The answer probably lies in a combination of ancient and modern factors.

An ancient fear

Throughout the Middle Ages, Herefordshire was very much frontier territory with the Welsh, like the Apaches always being seen as a potential enemy capable of making devastating attacks. In the 11th century Gruffudd ap Llywelyn had sacked Hereford itself and there were many later raids besides. In the 15th century Owain Glyndŵr had marched his army through the county. Even in the 16th century there was a fear that the Welsh could support a Spanish invasion. Thus, the fact that there was a large native Welsh population in Herefordshire itself was always a source of worry to the authorities there because of the possibility that they might support their more westerly brethren. Consequently, there would have been a general policy of Anglicisation coupled with attempts to play down the county's Welshness. Perhaps, like the woman from Cinderford in the Forest of Dean, they were told to believe that although they spoke Welsh, they were really English now. The real Welsh were a wild and savage people from the hills and not like them at all. However, such measures were only partially effective before the great social and industrial changes of the19th and 20th centuries.

The re-emergence of Wales

After the Act of Union of 1536, Wales and the Marcher lordships were 'pacified' and there was little difference on either side of what is now the border between England and Wales. Wales had technically ceased to exist under the Act, and so too had the Welsh language. However, although English was the official language of justice and administration on both sides of this 'border', the change was only gradual, until the coming of widespread English-only education and the rural depopulation mentioned by Matthews, in the 19th century. For practical purposes, Welsh was still used in certain spheres such as religion and rural trading, neither of which recognised any boundary. Also, it was still often the language of the hearth in many Herefordshire homes.

The 20th century witnessed an increasing divergence in perceived identity on each side of the border. Whilst, as a result of the pressures on it, the Welsh language receded westwards during the course of the 19th century, in Wales itself, there was a growing feeling of national identity. New institutions began to appear, in a trend that was to continue into and throughout the 20th century which ended with the establishment of the National Assembly of Wales.

The coming of radio and television in the 20th century media revolution has also meant that whilst Wales has developed its own public media systems, Herefordshire has become more and more integrated into the West Midland region of England, dominated by Birmingham. Local news and weather etc. on TV and radio and in the press tend to reflect this regional identity, with only a little time given to local variety. Similarly, the pressures of the National Curriculum in schools has left little time to teach Herefordshire school-children about the rich diversity of the county they live in. Rather, when they are taught anything about local history, only aspects of the county's place in English history are covered. To paraphrase Kearney 'Hereford in Wales' has been lost by projecting the modern county boundary back to the earliest times.

Rediscovering the heritage

Today there is no threat of invasion by the wild Welsh of the hills, and no longer any danger involved in the people of western Hereford finding out about 'Hereford in Wales' and their Welsh roots. These roots are deep and the ancient kingdoms of Ergyng and Ewyas are full of reminders of past glories, from Caradog and his Silures to Glyndŵr and his daughters; from Dyfrig and his saints to Howell Harris and his Methodists.

Herefordshire people in these areas with a strong Welsh legacy could find rediscovering their identity a fascinating business. At the very least they would become aware that they have this wonderfully rich border past and that this past could well be worth more than they realise. In the Introduction, I made a brief comparison of Herefordshire and Cornwall. Cornwall celebrates its Celtic past and makes a lot of tourist money from being different. So why can't Herefordshire be the same, nurturing its Welsh traditions as well as its English ones and promoting itself as an Anglo-Welsh Marcher County with its own unique blend of traditions? Perhaps it could even put up a few bilingual tourist signs and make Welsh language lessons available in evening classes. Why not?

Booklist (for chapter 12, and Conclusion):

Wales and her Language, by John E. Southall, pub. by J.E. Southall, 149, Dock St., Newport, Mon. and E. Hicks, London, 1892.

Protestant Dissenters in Wales, 1639-1689, by Geraint H. Jenkins, pub. by Cardiff University of Wales Press, 1992.

Howell Harris and the Dawn of Revival, by Richard Bennet (translated from Welsh by Gomer M. Roberts), pub. by the Evangelical Press of Wales, 1987 (original Welsh, 1909).

Hundred of Wormelow (upper division, Part I) by John Hobson Matthews ('Mab Cernyw'), Jarman & Carver, High Town, Hereford, 1912. As part of Collections towards the History and Antiquities of the County of Hereford, (in continuation of Duncumb's History).

The Welsh, their Language and Place Names in Archenfield and Oswestry, by B.G. Charles, in an article in the O'Donnell Lectures 'Angles and Britons', Cardiff University of Wales Press, 1963.

Portrait of the Wye Valley, by H.L.V. Fletcher, pub. Robert Hale, London, 1969.

A History of Modern Wales, by David Williams, pub. by John Murray, London, 2nd edition, 1977.

History of Wales, Vol.IV, The Foundations of Modern Wales, 1642-1780, Geraint H. Jenkins, Clarendon Press, Oxford/University of Wales Press, 1987.

The British Isles, A history of Four Nations, by Hugh Kearney, Cambridge University Press, 1989.

Appendix 1

A Gazetteer of Welsh place-names in western Herefordshire

Ergyng & Ewyas
Deu wur laweys went huc coyt
The two true sleeves of Gwent uwch Coed
From a Medieval poem

Many of the names in western Herefordshire are very old and appear in the 12th century Book of Llandaf, much of which material comes from much older sources. The following list is only a sample of present day Welsh place-names there. It is by no means exhaustive. To compile it I used the Ordnance Survey One Inch to One Statute Mile, Sheet 142, Hereford, and the adjacent 1¼ inch to the mile Landranger maps, 161 and 162. Had I used a larger scale map, far more names would have become apparent. For example, in square 53.18, only *'Trewen'* shows up on the 1 inch map, yet a larger scale map (2½ inch) also shows an *'Upper Trewen'* and a *'Little Trewen'* in the same square. In all probability, I've also missed a few names myself. Even so, two facts emerge. Firstly the greatest concentration of obviously Welsh names is west of the River Dore in Ewyas and in the central and southern parts of Archenfield. The lowest concentration is in the old Webtree Hundred, i.e. the northern part of Archenfield, along the Wye from Moccas to Hereford and near Hereford itself. However, even here there are apparently English place-names that are either corruptions of Welsh ones or are direct translations of them, e.g. **Dinedor**, 53.36, near the Wye and quite close to Hereford is clearly derived from Welsh *Din y dŵr, din* = fort and *dŵr* = water (or in this case river), i.e Fort near the river, taking its name from the old hillfort there.

Names of Welsh origin also occur in other parts of Hereford, Some, naturally are quite near the modern border, such as **Great Penllan,** 27.52, **Little Penllan,** 27.51 (*Penllan* = top of the church) and **Pentre Jack,** 27.50 (Jack's Village *). Others, like **Dilwyn**, 41.54 (*dil* = honeycomb; *wyn* = white; white honeycomb) are a bit further in. Yet others are at quite a distance from the modern border, e.g. **Upper Dinmore**, 48.50, and **Dinmore Manor,** at quite a distance from the modern border, e.g. **Upper Dinmore**, 48.50, and **Dinmore Manor**, near **Wellington**, 49.48 (which itself is derived from *'Llywelyn's town'*). *Din* = fort; more = *mawr* = big/great, i.e. great fort, *Pencombe*, 59.52, 4 miles SW of Bromyard; *pen* = top; coombe = *cwm* = valley i.e. top of the valley, and what about **Bromyard** itself, 65.54, in the north-east of the county. Even this could possibly be derived from Welsh and mean 'the breast of the fort', i.e. *brom* = breast; yard = *garth* = fort, see *'Penyard'*.

The high number of obviously Welsh farm names in Ewyas and the central and southern parts of Archenfield provides a good testimony to the survival of the Welsh language in these areas up until quite recent times. Definitely well into the 19th century, if not the 20th*.

Common elements in Welsh place-names

Aber = mouth or confluence of a river; *allt* = hillside; *bach* = small/little; *bron/brom* = breast; *bryn* = hill; *cefn* = ridge or back; *cil/kil/gil* = corner, retreat, nook; *coed* = wood, woods; *cwm* = valley; *du* (pronounced 'dee') = black; *dyffryn* = valley; *hen* = old; *hengoed* = old woods; *llan* = church/holy person's settlement, often but not always followed by a saint or holy person's name; *mawr* = big, major; *pen* = head/top/end; *pentre* = village; *pont* = bridge; *rhos* = moor, plain, heath, common; *ti/di* = thou/thy, a term of endearment sometimes put in front of a saint's name*; *tref/tre/dre* = the town/settlement/homestead of; *tŷ* = house; *y, yr, 'r* = the/of the.

Notes:. 1. B of Llan = Book of Llandaf. 2.The map references are the 1 kilometre Ordnance squares, of the large SO (100km) National Grid Square. The first number denotes the western edge of the square and the second number, the southern edge.

Welsh place-names in Archenfield (Wormelow and Webtree)

Aberhall, 52.24 – *aber*+hall = ***Hall by the confluence***
Altbough, 54.30 – *allt*+*bwch*(goat) = ***goathill***
Altwint, 52.30 – *allt*+wint = *wynt*(wind) = ***windy hillside***

Bagwy Llidiart, 45.26 – *bagwy* = point/tip+*llidiart* = gate = ***the gate by the point***
Ballingham, 57.31 – old form Badelingham, Lann Budgualan in B of Llan. The church is dedicated to St Dubricus/*Dyfrig*
Benarth Farm, 42.29 – *pen*+*arth*(bear) = ***bear's head farm***
Brom y Close, 51.28 – near Lanwarne

175

Bryngwyn, 48.30 – *bryn+gwyn* = *white hill*
Bryngwyn Hill, 47.29

Camdore Farm, 45.26 – *cam+dŵr* = crooked water, *winding stream farm* near Bagwy Llidiart
Carwendy, 46.25 – *caer* = fort; *wen* = white; *dŷ* = house = *house of the white fort*
Crac o Hill Farm, 46.31 – *crac* = angry/nasty. Similar to 'Crac Hill Farm', near Bridgend
Cwm, The, 49.17
Cwm Craig, 53.32 – near little Dewchurch; *cwm+craig* = *rocky valley*
Cwm Maddoc Farm, 47.20 – *Maddoc's valley farm*

Dewchurch (Little), 53.31 – A church dedicated to Dewi (St David)
Dewchurch (Much), 48.31 – Lann Deui Ros Cerion (the church of Dewi by Cerion's moor) in B of Llan
Dewsall, 48.33 – *Dewi*'s well, St David's well
Dinedor, 53.36 – *din* = fort, *dŵr* = water; *fort by the river/water*
Doward, Great, 54.16 – hill near Ganarew
Doward, Little, 53. 16 – The hillfort here is thought to have been Vortigern's stronghold destroyed by Emrys and Uther. Geoffrey of Monmouth calls the castle 'Genoreu' (Ganarew) and says that it is on a hill called 'Cloartius', in Erging, beside the Wye. As Cair Guorthigrin it is also a strong contender to be one of Nennius' 28 cities of the whole of Britain.

Some 2 miles north of Monmouth near Ganarew, but on the the other side of the A40, these two hills can be seen from the road. **'Doward'** is derived from Doy(or *Dwy*) = Two+*arth*. As *'arth'* is Welsh for 'bear' and is the root of King Arthur's name, local legend has led to a nearby cave being called 'Arthur's Cave'. However, in Welsh words following 'Doy/Dwy' often change their first letter (i.e. 'g' disappears). Thus *'arth'* could be *'garth'* = hillfort. Doward would then be the collective name for both hills (and their forts) i.e. Doy +*garth* = two hillforts, which seems more plausible than 'two bears'

Dyffryn, 41,32 – *valley*

Foy, 59.28* – shortened from Tifoy/*Tyfwy* = *Ti*+ *Moe/Mwy* (saint's name). Lanntiuoi in B of Llan. (*Ti* = Thou/Thy). B.G. Charles says that prefixing a particle *'ti'* (or *'dŷ'*) *'thŷ'* to a saints name was a common Celtic usage. See also 'Llandinabo'.

Gamber, The, 50.24 – *cam* = crooked = crooked/winding brook

Ganarew, 52.16 – In the Welsh version of Geoffrey of Monmouth's 12th century History of the Kings, it is called *Castell Goronw* = Goronw's Castle. Lanngunuarui in B.of Llan. Vortigern had his castle near here (see Little Doward, above).

Garren Brook, 51.22 – near Llangarron, from *garan* = a crane originally *'Nant Garan'*

Garway, 45.21 – Lanngarewi in B of Llan. The church of Guorvoe/*Gwrfwy*

Gillow Manor, 53.25 – half way between St Owens Cross and Michaelchurch, *gil* = retreat; *lwch* = pool; ***retreat by the pool***

Gwenherrion Farm, 51.18 – *gwen* = white

Hendre, 55.23 – Old settlement. Also, winter dwelling
Hentland, 54.26 – Henlann (*hen+llan* = old church) in B of

Llan. This is where St Dyfrig established a monastic college for over a thousand students.

Kentchurch, 41.25 – after Saint Cein. Lann Cein in the B of Llan. Still called Llankeyne in 1469

Kilforge House, 55.32 – kil/*cil* = nook/retreat

Killbreece, 52.23 – *cil+ab*(son of)+*rhys* = *The retreat of Rhys' son*

Kilpeck, 44.30 – Shortened from Lann Degui Cilpedic in the B of Llan, i.e. the church of Dewi (St David) in Cilpedic. Cilpedic (Kilpeck) = *cil*+Pedic i.e. *the retreat of St Pedic*

Kilreague Farm, 51.21 – *cil+yr*+ague(?)

Llancloudy, 49.20 – Lann Loudeu (Loudy) in the B of Llan, a disciple of Dyfrig

Llandinabo, 51.28* – Lann lunabiu in the B of Llan. Named after one of Dyfrig's disciples, lunabwy. *Llan+Ti*(thou)+lunabwy. See 'Foy'.

Llanerch Brook, 50.20 – *llan+erch*(speckled), *speckled church brook*

Llanfrother, 53.28

Llangarron, 53.21 – church named after the river, (*Nant*) Garren Brook. *Garan* = crane

Llangrove, 52.19 – *church in the grove*

Llangunnock, 51.23 – Gunnock or Cunnock, perhaps *Cynog's church*

Llangunnock Bridge, 50.22

Llangunnock Brook, 51.22

Llangunville Farm, 49.16

Llanithog Farm, 43.26

Llanrothal, 48.17 – Lann Ridol in B of Llan

Llantywaun Brook, 49.21 – *tŷ* = house, *waun* = meadow;

brook called after the church of the house in the meadow

Llanwarne, 50.28 – *wern* = swamp or alder grove = church in the alder grove

Madley, 42.38 – *mat*(good)+*le*(place) = 'the good place' in the Book of Llan. This was St Dyfrig's first church.

Marlas, 43.29 – blue earth/clay?

Michaelchurch, 52.25 – English rendering of Lann Mihacgel cil luc in the B of Llan. i.e. The Church of Saint Michael by Cil lwch (see Gillow)

Moccas, 35.42 – In the Book of Llan this was St Dyfrig's new settlement (after Hentland). A place where he would find a white sow and her young, and where the Wye was full of fish. *Moch-rhos* (the pig's heath) became Moccas.

Mynd, The, 47.29 – *mynd/mynydd* = hill or mountain

Mynde Wood, 47.29 – the wood by the hill

Old Hendre, 49.26 – *hen+dre* = **old settlement** (see page 161)

Penalt, 57.29 – *pen+allt* = **top of the hillside**, near King's Caple

Penblaith Farm, 49.19 – *pen+blaidd*(wolf) = **wolf's head**

Pencraig, 56.20 – *pen+craig* = **top of the rock/crag**

Pencoyd, 51.26 – *pen+coed* = **end of the woods**

Pengethley, 54.25 – *pen+gelli* = **top/end of the grove**

Pennarstone, 55.28 – *Pennar* is an old Welsh name

Penrose, 48.21 – *pen+rhos* = **top of the moor**

Penyard, 61.22 – *pen+garth*, *Peniarth* in Welsh = **top of the fortified hill**

Pontrilas, 39.27 – *pont+tri*(three)+*glas*(blue i.e. water) = **bridge by the three waters** (i.e. the Dore, Worm, Dulas rivers)

Red Rail, 54.28 – near Llanfrother, 'red' here could easily be *'rhyd'* = ford, and rail could be yr *heol* = the road; i.e. *the ford of the road*. After all Red Rail is near the Wye. cf Redruth in Cornwall; red = ford; ruth = red (*rhudd* in W)

Ross on Wye, 60.24 – *Rhosan yr Wy* in Welsh, *rhosan* is a variety of *rhos* = moor/plain = *moor by the Wye*

Rhydd, The, 47.32 – *rhydd* = free

St Devereux parish, 45.32 – St Devereux = *St Dyfrig*/Dubricus

St Weonards, 49.24 – Lann Santguainerth (Saint *Gwainerth* or *Gwenarth*). In the Book of Llan.

Sellack, 56.27 – shortened from Lann Suluc a familiar form of *Suliau*, or *Tysulio* (*Tŷ* = *Ti* = thou in front of saint's name) to whom the church is still dedicated.

Treaddow, 54.24 – *adwy* = gap; *homestead by/in the gap*

Trebandy Farm, 54.20 – *pandy* = fulling mill (to process wool)

Trebunfrey, 52.22 – bunfrey = Humfrey = Norman's name; *Humfrey's Town/settlement*

Tredunnock, 52.20

Tre Essey, 50.21

Tre Essey Cross, 50.21

Trelasdee Farm, 50.23 – tre+*las*(blue)+*du*(black) = *the farm of blue black town*

Trelough, 43.31

Tremahaid, 49.18

Trereece, 52.20 – *Rhys' town/settlement*

Treribble, 51.22

Tretire, 52.23 – tre+*tir*(land), *town of the land?*

Trevase Farm, 51.25

Treverven, 54.20

Treville, 43.31 – *tryfal* = triangle of land in the fork of two rivers

Trewarne, 52.17 – *tre+wern* = ***town by the swamp/alder grove***

Trewaugh, 51.22

Trewen, 53.18 – *tre+wen*(white) = ***white town***

Treworgan, 51.19 – possibly ***Morgan's town***

Trippenkennet, 50.22 – *tri*(three)+*pen*(head)+kennet (*cerrig*? = rocks) = possibly ***'the tops of the three rocks'***, referring to some local geographical feature.

Velindra, 49.22 – velin (mill)+*dre* = ***mill town***

Walford, 58.20 – to the south of Ross, on opposite bank of Wye to Pencraig. Walford takes its name from 'Welsh ford'. The Roman road from Monmouth to Ariconium crossed near here.

Welsh Bicknor, 59.17 – in contrast to English Bicknor on the opposite bank of the Wye. It was Lann Custenhin = Constantine's church in the B of Llan.

Welsh Newton, 50.17

Worm Bridge, 41.31

Wormelow, 49.30 – takes its name from the River Worm, which is called 'Guormui' in the B of Llan. This would be 'Gwyrmwy' or 'the winding river' in today's Welsh. Wormelow was also the name of the medieval hundred.

Worm River, 40.29

Welsh place-names in Ewyas

Abbey Dore, 38.30 – dore is derived from Welsh *'dŵr'* = water. Not French D'or = gold
Arthur's Stone, 31.42 – burial chamber, near Dorestone

Blaen, 27.33 – *blaen* = summit/top end
Blaen Olchon, 27.33 – top end of the Olchon Valley
Bryn, 33.29 – *bryn* = hill
Bwlch Farm, 26.41 – *bwlch* = mountain pass

Cae Mawr, 29.38 – *cae* = field; *mawr* = big; *big field*
Cefn, 36.30 – on the ridge, near Abbey Dore
Cefn Farms, 28.37 – farms on the ridge
Cefn Keist, 31.35 – Keist ridge
Cefn Hill, 27.38
Clodock, 32.27 – after St Clydawg
Coed Major, 26.27 – *coed* = woods
Coed Poeth,32.35 – *poeth* = hot; *hot woods*
Coed Robin,29.36 – *Robin's wood*
Cwarelau, 34.31 – *quarries*
Cwmbologne, 35.29 – possibly 'bologne' may be a corruption of something else.
Cwm Brook, 37.26 – *cwm* = *valley*
Cwmcoched Lower, 25.32 – *coched* derived from *coch* = red; *red valley*
Cwm Farm, 32.38
Cwm Farm Upper, 30.33
Cwm Farms, 30.31
Cwm Steps, 30.32

Dineterwood, 38.27 – *din* = fort
Duffryn, 41.31 – *dyffryn* = *valley*

Herefordshire, the Welsh Connection

Dolward Farm, 33.36 – *dôl* = meadow/dale

Fedw, 36.27 – *bedw* = *birch trees*

Gilfach, 34.34 – *little nook*
Greidol, 34.27 – *dôl* = meadow; 'grei' could be derived from *'creigiau'* = rocks, i.e. *rocky meadow*
Goytre Upper, 35.24 – goytre = *winter settlement*
Gwyrlodydd, 34.32 – the plural for *'gwyrlod'*, another word for meadow.

Llancillo, 36.25 – *the church in Lo's nook*
Llan Farm, 31.42 – *church farm*
Llanover, 31.32 – *Over's church*
Llanrosser, 29.37 – *Rosser's church*
Llanveynoe, 30.31 – St Beuno's church, in the Olchon Valley
Llanwonog, 32.29 – *Wonog's church*, near Longtown
Llan y Coed, 27.42 – church of the woods
Llyndu, 33.31 – *llyn* = lake; *du* = black; *black lake*

Maerdy, 30.37 – *maer* = steward/reeve; *dŷ* = house; *Steward's House*
Maerdy, 34.30 – near Lower Maes Coed, Dulas Valley
Maes Coed Lower, 34.30 – *field of the woods*; *maes* = field. In the Dulas Valley.
Maes Coed Middle, 33.33
Maes Coed Upper, 33.34
Mynydd Myrddin, 33.27 – *Myrddin/Merlin's Mountain*

Nant y Bar, 28.40 – *nant* = stream; *the bar stream*

Parc y Meirch, 25.37 – *meirch* = stallions; *Park of the Stallions*

Pentre Farms, 33.43 – *pentre* = village; *Village Farms*, near Bredwadine

Pentre Higgin, 25.39 – *Higgin's village*

Pentwyn, 30.36 – *pen* = top; *twyn* = hillock/knoll; *top of the knoll*

Pen y Lan, 33.27 – *lan/glan* = bank; *top of the bank*

Penylan Farm, 38.26

Pen y Moor Farm, 31.43 – *top of the moor*

Pen y Park, 30.38 – *top of the park*

Pontynys, 32.28 – *pont* = bridge; *ynys* = island; *bridge of the island*, in Longtown

Red Daren, 29.30 – red = *rhyd* = a ford; *Daren's Ford*

Straddle – From the Welsh *'ystrad'* = wide valley or vale. This was the old name for the *Golden Valley*, e.g. as in Monnington Straddle, now Monnington Court (38.36), where Glyndŵr's daughter Alice lived.

Tir Bill Farm, 29.31 – *tir* = land; *the farm on Bill's land*

Tre-cadifer, 33.35 – Cadi is Welsh for Katy. *Fer* = short; *little Katy's place*

Trelach Ddu, 29.30 – *lach* = lash/whip; *ddu* (pron. Thee); *settlement of The black whip*

Trelanden, 33.29 – *lan* = bank; *settlement on the bank of the Den* (or Landen could be a name), near Longtown

Trelough, 43.31

Tremorithic, 36.31 – *'mor'* could be *mawr* = big, and Rithic could be someone's name, i.e. Big Rithic's place

Trenant Brook, 33.37 – *nant* = brook

Trewern, 32.30 – *wern* = marsh/alder grove; *settlement in the marsh*

Turnant, 30.28 – *tur* is probably *'tir'* = land; *land by the brook*

Twrn y Beddau, 24.38 – *Turn of the graves*, ancient monument
Tŷ bach, 32.30 – *little house*, in the Monnow Valley
Tŷ Canol, 34.27 – canol = middle; *middle house*
Tŷ Cradoc, 32.32 – *Caradoc's House*
Tŷ Mawr, 32.26 – *mawr* = big; *big house*
Tŷ Uchaf, 28.39 – *uchaf* = highest; *highest house*

Vro, 38.26 – v = b, *bro* = land, but could be short for *'bron'* = breast

Wainherbert, 33.32 – *waun* = meadow; *Herbert's meadow*
Wern Ddu, 34.29 – *wern* = swamp/alder grove, *ddu* (pron. thee) = black = *Black swamp*

Welsh place-names in the old Marcher Lordships

The existence of a cluster of Welsh place-names, mostly farms and tiny hamlets to the north of Archenfield and Ewyas, in the hills on the Herefordshire side of the border between Kington and the Wye Valley at Clifford (i.e. in the old Marcher lordships of Huntington, Whitney, Wynforten, Eardisley and Clifford itself. See map), also argues well for the survival of the Welsh language in this part of the border into the 19th century. Below is a list with map references, taken from OS Landranger 148, 1¼ inch map;

Burnt Hengoed, 26.52 – (built on the land of the) burnt old woods

Cefn, 25.49 – probably built on a ridge

Cwmmau Farmhouse, 27.51 – *cwmmau* = valleys, 17th farmhouse, owned by N.T. and open to the public. In Brilley parish.

Great Penlan, 27.52 – *pen* = top; *lan* = church: possible location of old church.

Hengoed, 24.52 – *hengoed* = old woods

Little Merthyr, 26.48 – *merthyr* = martyr

Little Penlan, 27.51

Llanarrow Cottage, 25.52 – *llan* = church; arrow could be *'garw'* = rough; could be named after another cottage on the river Arrow

Llanhendry Farm, 27.50 – *llan* = church; *hen* = old; 'dry' could originally have been 'tŷ' i.e. ***church of the old house farm***

Pen Brilley, 23.48 – top of Brilley, Brilley parish is north of the Wye valley

Pentre Coed, 28.49 – village in the woods

Pentregrove, 23.48 – village in the grove

Pentre Jack, 28.50 – Jack's village

Pentre Miley, 24.49 – Miley's village

Pentwyn Camp, 22.48 – old hillfort

Pontvaen, 23.43 – *faen* = *maen* = stone, ***Stone Bridge***, close to the border near Clifford

Rhydspence, 24.47 – *rhyd* = ford; ***Spencer's Ford***; straddling the border, near Clifford

Trenewydd, 25.50 – *newydd* = new; ***new town/settlement***

Wern, 24.48 – (g)*wern* = wet-land/swamp
Welshwood Farm, 27.49
Welson, Lower, 29.50 – possibly Welshton/Welshtown?
Welson, Upper, 29.51

In addition to this group, there is a thin scattering of Welsh names throughout the county, e.g. Penrhos, 31.56, near Kington (spelt Ceintun in Welsh), Dilwyn, 41.54, The Rhyse, 35.57, near Pembridge (Pem could be Pen), Wigmore (wig = wood; more = *mawr* = big/great, i.e. Great Wood, 41.69, etc. Even the River Arrow could be named from 'garw' meaning rough (i.e. fast running).

A final reminder of the Welsh connection with Herefordshire is the fact that both Hereford and Leominster have Welsh versions of their names, respectively **Henffordd** (*hen* = old; *ffordd* = road i.e. the old road) and **Llanllieni** (*llan+llieni; llieni* a plural of *lleian* = nun, probably referring to the convent that was there and the linen habits of the nuns.

*Note on 'di/tŷ' = *thy/thou. B.G. Charles says that Foy is derived from 'Lanntiuoi' after the saint Tifoy or Tyfwy in the Book of Llandaf and that it is a "hypocoristic" name formed by prefixing* 'ti' (dŷ) = thŷ, *in accordance with Celtic usage, to the name 'Moy'. The same saints name, as Tyfei, is found in Llandyfei (Lamphey in English) in Pembrokeshire.*

Booklist:
The Lives of the Welsh Saints, by G.H. Doble, edited by D. Simon Evans, Cardiff University of Wales Press, 1971.
The Welsh, their Language and Placenames in Archenfield and Oswestry, by B.G. Charles, as part of the O'Donnell Lectures, 'Angles and Britons' published by The University of Wales Press, 1963.

Hundred of Wormelow, by John Hobson Matthews (Mab Cernwy), Jakeman & Carver, Hereford, 1912.

Ordnance Survey Maps, Hereford, Sheet 142 One Inch Map; Landranger 162, Gloucester & Forest of Dean (2cm = 1 km or 1¼ inches = 1 mile); Landranger 161, Abergavenny & the Black Mountains (2cm = 1km); Landranger 148, Presteigne & Hay on Wye area (2cm = 1km); and for comparison the 2½ inch Outdoor Leisure Map of the Wye Valley and Forest of Dean (i.e. square 53.18)

Cymru, Map yn y Gymraeg, Cyhoeddiadau Stad, Y Drenewydd, Powys.

A History of the Kings of Britain, by Geoffrey of Monmouth, translated by Lewis Thorpe, Penguin Books, 1966.

Vortigern Studies, Caer Guorthegirn, internet article by Robert Vermaat.

History from the Sources, 'Nennius', general editor John Morris, Phillimore, 1980.

Appendix 2

The following items are examples of contemporary links between Wales and Herefordshire

'Giant Welsh Dragon slays Hereford rugby protest'

The Western Mail, on 22nd of September 1999, reported that *'A towering Welsh Dragon was to be erected in an English border city despite a roar of disapproval from residents'*.

However, in spite of receiving planning permission to erect a 20ft high dragon with a 7 metre wing span, Hereford Welsh Club faced strong resistance from local residents.

Polish born sculptor Walenty Pytel was commissioned by the Club to make the steel statue. He agreed to make it at cost price as a Millennium gift to the city and its Welsh inhabitants.

A leader of the protestors, Mark Rone the licensee of a nearby public house, *The Treacle Mine*, suggested that Hereford folk were proud to be English and might be provoked into anti Welsh acts by the sight of the dragon. He also suggested that were an English pub in Cardiff to erect an English Rose sculpture, it would soon attract the attentions of 'The Sons Of Glyndŵr' (a direct action group). He added that the dragon would be an eyesore and a traffic hazard and suggested a smaller version in the garden of the Club. He finished by saying that the protest was not anti Welsh and that many of his customers were Welsh.

Footnote: When I wrote to the Club in 2002, I found that the giant dragon project had been dropped.

'Sian Phillips to unveil Glyndŵr statue'

On the 15th September 2001The Western Mail reported that the famous actress Sian Phillips was, on the following day, to unveil a memorial to commemorate the forced exile and death of Owain Glyndŵr's daughter Catrin and three of her children, at Cannon Street Gardens, in London.

The project was organised by Isabel Monnington-Taylor, a descendent of the *Herefordshire Monningtons*. One of Glyndŵr's daughters had married into the Monnington family and reports suggest that he may be buried at Monnington Court.

We decided to build a memorial to commemorate Catrin Glyndŵr in London following the activities commemorating the 600th anniversary of the uprising which started in Wales last year. This is an opportunity for us in London to remember Catrin Glyndŵr and the suffering she and her children endured during this turbulent period in the history of Wales.

Catrin and her children were captured when Harlech castle fell to English forces in 1409 and sent to the Tower of London where they died in unknown circumstances four years later. Their burial site is believed to have been the old St Swithin's graveyard in London which is thought to be under the site of the present Cannon Street Gardens.

The memorial has been carved from Gelligaer bluestone and depicts a flowing line leading from a stone base to a bronze tip, suggesting the figures of a mother protecting her child. It was designed by the Welsh artist, Nic Stradling-John and created by Richard Renshaw who is based near Crickhowell. Mr Stradling-John said that the memorial also represented all women and children who had suffered during war. *'The statue is about the spirit of strength to regrow after the tragic periods people go through'.*

Two inscriptions by the writer and poet Menna Elfyn appear on the stone, one in Welsh and the other in English.

Sian Phillips said that she was honoured to be asked to unveil the stone, and said, *'The memorial will create a focal point in London for people with Welsh connections'.*

'Prince's Welsh Marches revival project to start next month'

On Saturday 11th January 2003, The Western Mail reported that a multi-million pound project by the Duchy of Cornwall to revive a derelict **900 acre estate in the Welsh marches at Harewood End**, some 5 miles west of Ross, on the A49 to Hereford, was set to begin in February 2003. The Prince of Wales, who is also the Duke of Cornwall, was 'planning a country house dwelling as the centre-piece of the scheme, set beside the picturesque River Wye in Herefordshire'.

The estate was bought by the Duchy of Cornwall in

May 2000. Because its previous owners could no longer afford its upkeep.

The late Georgian country house had been demolished with the help of the SAS in 1959. However, next to where the house stood there are a Grade II listed stable block and courtyard and an imposing Grade II listed chapel.

The project, headed by Builth Wells based architect Craig Hamilton whose work had impressed the Prince, will probably take ten years, with the first stage focusing on restoring five cottages and three outbuildings at Home Farm. The next step would involve the renovation of a cluster of buildings at Grange Farm to provide houses and workshops.

Reports that the estate could become a future home for Princes William and Harry were strongly denied by David Curtis, the Duchy's land manager in Herefordshire. He said that the redevelopment was to aid rural regeneration with the project being expected to revive a valley that was at present full of derelict farmsteads and cottages. The country house would be on the rental market.

Some Sporting Links *(as reported in 'This is Herefordshire' on the net)*

Swimming: Leominster Kingfishers Swimming Club is in the *Mid Wales League*. Reported to have beaten arch rivals Ludlow into second place and Welshpool into third, on Thurs. 26 Sept. 2002.

Athletics: Hereford and County AC competed in the fourth *Celtic Manor South East Wales League* meeting at Aberdare on August 12, 2001.

Football: In 1958 Hereford United beat second division Cardiff at Ninian Park in the Welsh FA Cup Competition. John Charles became manager in the 1965/66 season. In 1968 Hereford was in the Welsh Cup Final at Cardiff. United lost 6-1 on aggregate.

Recruited for the League of Wales

It was reported early in May 2002 that Hereford would provide three players for Wales' semi professional squad to take part in the Home Countries' Internationals later in the year. Hereford United's Paul Parry and Tony James would be joined by striker Gavin Williams to 'fly the flag for Wales'.

Hockey: Herefordshire men's hockey teams are in the *West of England and South Wales Men's League.*